First published in Great Britain 2023 by Farshore
An imprint of HarperCollins*Publishers*
1 London Bridge Street, London SE1 9GF
www.farshore.co.uk

HarperCollins*Publishers*
Macken House, 39/40 Mayor Street Upper,
Dublin 1, D01 C9W8, Ireland

Written by Tom Stone
Additional Illustrations by George Lee
Special thanks to Sherin Kwan, Alex Wiltshire, Jay Castello, Kelsey Ranallo and Milo Bengtsson

This book is an original creation by Farshore

ISBN 978 0 00 853743 2
Printed in Italy
1

ONLINE SAFETY FOR YOUNGER FANS

Spending time online is great fun! Here are a few simple rules to help younger fans stay safe and
keep the internet a great place to spend time:
- Never give out your real name – don't use it as your username.
- Never give out any of your personal details.
- Never tell anybody which school you go to or how old you are.
- Never tell anybody your password except a parent or a guardian.
- Be aware that you must be 13 or over to create an account on many sites.
Always check the site policy and ask a parent or guardian for permission before registering.
- Always tell a parent or guardian if something is worrying you.
Stay safe online. Any website addresses listed in this book are correct at the time of going to print.
However, Farshore is not responsible for content hosted by third parties. Please be aware that online
content can be subject to change and websites can contain content that is unsuitable for children.
We advise that all children are supervised when using the internet.

Stay safe online. Farshore is not responsible for content hosted by third parties.

All information and stats are based on Minecraft: Bedrock Edition.

MINECRAFT

MOBSPOTTER'S
ENCYCLOPEDIA

■

THE ULTIMATE GUIDE TO
THE MOBS OF MINECRAFT

CONTENTS

IT'S TIME FOR ADVENTURE

Welcome to Minecraft, a place where exploration and discovery is rewarded with the most spectacular sights and magnificent mobs you could ever see. Many are neutral and some are passive but, unfortunately, lots are hostile and you will need to be prepared – especially when it comes to the dangerous dimensions of the Nether and the End. There's never been a better time to get started, so let's meet the hosts that will be guiding you along this wild adventure!

MEET THE EXPLORERS

ADDIE VENTURE

No one has spent more time wandering the flatlands than Addie Venture. Her expertise in common mobs is unrivalled, so there is no better guide to the early-game creatures you'll encounter when you first start to explore the Overworld.

DWIGHT WALKER

This famed explorer is known for his desire to discover every last location in the Overworld. He is never in one place for long enough to tell of his travels, so we're thrilled that he found the time to share his experiences with you for this book.

DR DORA SETTLEWELL

After finishing her studies in Overworld cultures, Dr Settlewell set out to study villages. She is welcomed into communities, where she spends time getting to know her new neighbours.

HEIDI PEAKS

A fearless explorer raised in a remote mountain village, Heidi learned to climb before she could talk! She has scaled all of the highest jagged peaks in the Overworld.

RILEY WAVERIDER

Growing up on the water, Riley soon developed a love of being submerged. Their catchphrase, 'a day on land is a day wasted', explains why they are always underwater.

AMELIA NETHERHEART

Brilliant, brave and bizarre are the three words most often used to describe Amelia Netherheart. Her survival skills in the Nether had never been witnessed ... until now.

PROFESSOR ED PORTALE

The Professor, as he likes to be known, is an explorer of dimensions unlike any other. Often disappearing for months on end, he is a survival specialist and is sharing his experiences in the End for the first time.

BEGINNERS

Hi there! I'm Addie Venture, and I couldn't be more excited to be your guide to the mobs you'll meet as you begin your Overworld adventures! True, I don't have any 'qualifications' or 'formal survival training', or 'any idea what I'm talking about' ... but trust me! I'm gonna be a GREAT guide. I've hugged every passive mob, respectfully nodded at every neutral mob, and been defeated by every hostile mob! Er, strictly for research purposes, obvs! Can't tell the difference between a sheep and a creeper? Neither could I. But hundreds of disastrous hugs later, now I can – and I'm gonna pass that knowledge on to you. Let's turn the page and get started!

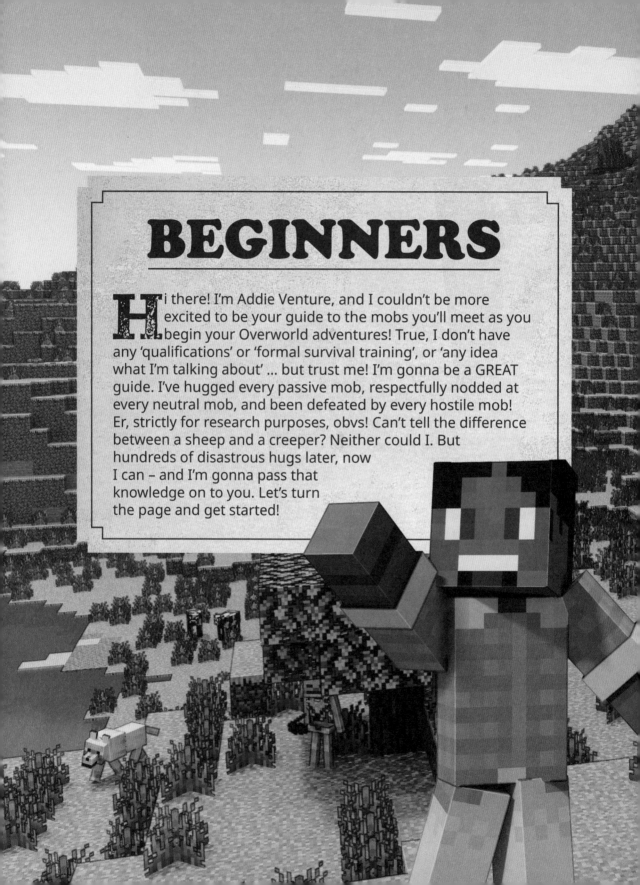

CHICKEN

At first glance, the chicken seems to be one of the unluckier mobs in the Overworld. Plenty of predators have this poor poultry in their sights and, given that it can't fly, its wings initially seem about as useful as concrete parachutes. However, it can still flap those wings enough to avoid taking fall damage! That's fortunate, as they're often chased by resourceful adventurers, keen to hunt them for their many drops.

> *Please ignore the MEAN statement above, because the chicken is way too adorable to be hunted! Fine, it's a great source of food, but for vegetarians like myself, it's a much better source of clucking companionship! I can see why farmers like them, though, because these yellow-beaked beauties can only jump one block high. That means they can't rudely hop over your fences. I'm looking at you, rabbits! The baby chicken is even cuter. When I first saw one on the plains, I vowed never to wash my eyes again. True story!*

HABITAT

Chickens can be found across grassy biomes, such as the plains, windswept hills, grove, taiga, forest, jungles and swamps. So if you're exploring a green biome and are in need of a meal, keep your eyes peeled for a chicken (sorry, Addie!) Remember to cook it first.

Plains

Windswept hills

Grove

Taiga

Forest

Jungle

Swamp

■ *A chicken next to an egg, baffling Overworld philosophers for centuries.*

MOB NOTES

BEHAVIOUR: Chickens wander aimlessly, but will come to you if you are holding certain seeds. They always flee from the attacks of ocelots, untamed cats and foxes.
DROPS: Adults will usually drop raw chicken and are likely to drop a feather or two – a vital ingredient for the crafting of arrows.

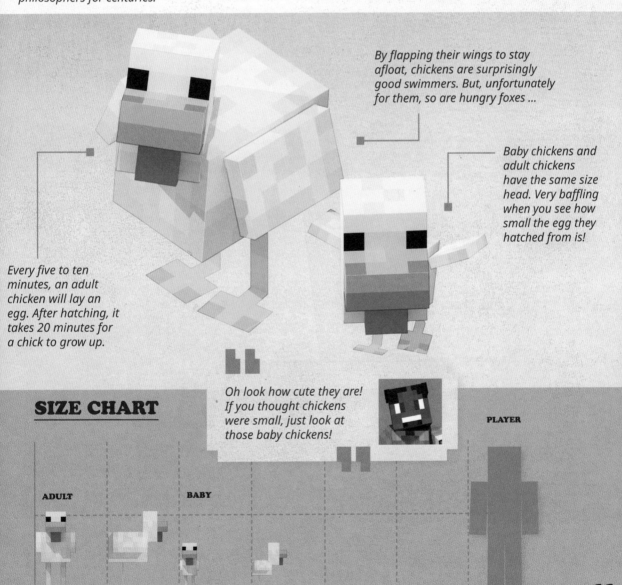

By flapping their wings to stay afloat, chickens are surprisingly good swimmers. But, unfortunately for them, so are hungry foxes ...

Baby chickens and adult chickens have the same size head. Very baffling when you see how small the egg they hatched from is!

Every five to ten minutes, an adult chicken will lay an egg. After hatching, it takes 20 minutes for a chick to grow up.

SIZE CHART

Oh look how cute they are! If you thought chickens were small, just look at those baby chickens!

PLAYER

ADULT

BABY

COW

This mooing milk factory is a favourite of any aspiring farmer. Offering leather and beef as well as milk, the cow is a resource-rich mob that loves eating wheat and being hand-fed by adventurers. You'll have plenty of 'beef' with this mob ... but in a good way!

> When I'm not exploring, I LOVE to bake. But you don't want to try baking cakes without milk in Minecraft (trust me, I found this out the hard way). That's why I keep a couple of cute cows outside my home! In exchange for their milk, I feed them wheat. Did you know that cows will only chow down on wheat if you're holding it? Some might find such behaviour a bit demanding, but I personally think it's affectionate! Besides, some hands-on feeding time with these spotted cuties feels like a small price to pay for keeping my cakes nice and edible.

HABITAT

You won't have to travel far to find a cow. They're common in plains, jungles, forests, swamps, extreme hills, and also villages (but can someone please warn them that BUTCHERS reside in these villages?). They're also one of the larger passive mobs, so it won't take you long to spot one on your travels!

Plains · Jungle · Forest · Swamp · Extreme hills

■ *A cow being milked by an adventurer. Don't forget your bucket!*

While they are known for mooing, cows sometimes give off huffing sounds, too. The most passive-aggressive mob in the Overworld? Possibly.

You'll need a bucket to get milk from a cow. Which makes sense. Otherwise, you'd just be wasting good milk and making the blocks beneath it all soggy. No one wants that.

If you're holding wheat within five blocks of a cow, it will follow you. Good to keep in mind if you're trying to lure one to your farm.

SIZE CHART

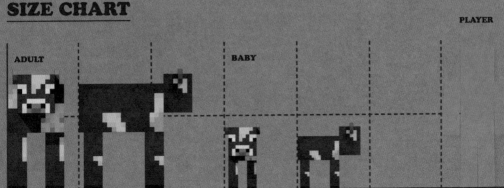

ADULT

BABY

PLAYER

PIG

Adorable on the outside and nutritious on the inside, the pig is popular with adventurers looking for a cute companion, trotter-based transport, or a tasty treat. This pastel pink mob is significantly less popular during thunderstorms, as anyone who's seen one struck by lightning will tell you. Assuming they survived to tell the tale ...

What is pink, oinks and has a curly tail? That's right: me getting thrown out of a recent costume party! Apparently oinking loudly at other guests is 'bad party etiquette'? I went as a pig because this superb swine is one of my favourite mobs. I'll begrudgingly admit that pigs are a great source of porkchops ... but wouldn't you rather hop on a pig's back and go for a LITERAL piggyback ride? Of course you would. Wait, you'd still rather eat it? Arghhh! At least let me get down from its back first!

HABITAT

Pigs love grass and can be found in almost all the grassy biomes, except for meadows, snowy plains and wooded badlands. They're a common mob and because of their delightful shade of pink, you'll be able to spot them from some distance.

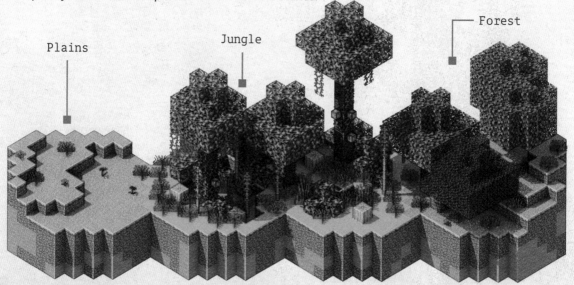

Plains   Jungle   Forest

■ *A pig in a thunderstorm? Turn to page 144 to see why this could be bad news!*

MOB NOTES

BEHAVIOUR: These peaceful animals can be found slowly roaming the Overworld, and will only up their pace if harmed.
AFRAID OF: It's safe to assume they're afraid of lightning, based on the outcome.
DROPS: Pigs will always drop at least one raw porkchop, which will be a cooked porkchop if defeated by fire. Tasty!

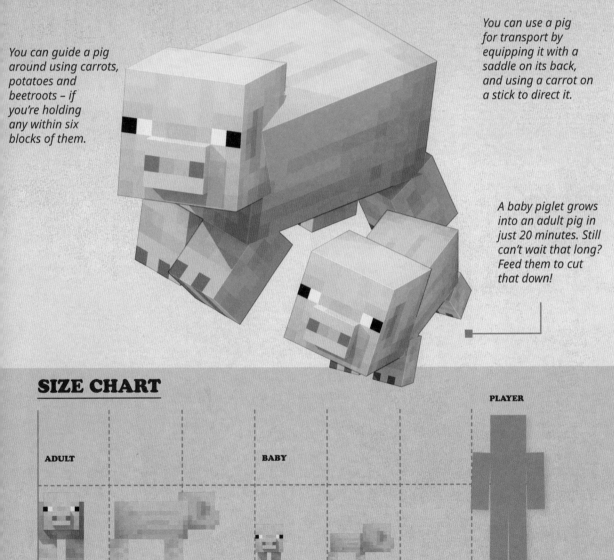

You can guide a pig around using carrots, potatoes and beetroots – if you're holding any within six blocks of them.

You can use a pig for transport by equipping it with a saddle on its back, and using a carrot on a stick to direct it.

A baby piglet grows into an adult pig in just 20 minutes. Still can't wait that long? Feed them to cut that down!

SIZE CHART

PLAYER

ADULT

BABY

SHEEP

Acommon mob that is coated in one of the most vital resources in the entire Overworld, you'll need to find a sheep or three if you want the wool to craft a bed (and you REALLY want to craft a bed – unless you want to risk meeting the mob on page 54). Luckily, sheep can't resist any wheat you're holding and they're super easy to farm – plus they bleat pleasantly, too.

> *How could I not adore a mob that looks like a little walking cloud? But be careful counting these while exploring. I can't tell you how many times I've fallen asleep doing that and woken up to find several skeletons using me for target practice (OK, I could actually tell you, but it's embarrassing and I don't want to). I've spent many a relaxing afternoon shearing sheep, only to notice the sun is dropping and I better hurry up if I want to craft a bed in time. I love that these woollen wonders drop up to three times more wool if you shear them instead of attacking them – a good reason to be a peaceful mobspotter!*

HABITAT

Sheep love chowing down on grass and can often be seen on grass blocks in almost every biome. They have even been known to appear in butcher houses in villages. Which, er, seems HIGHLY unwise for their long-term survival ...

In most grassy biomes

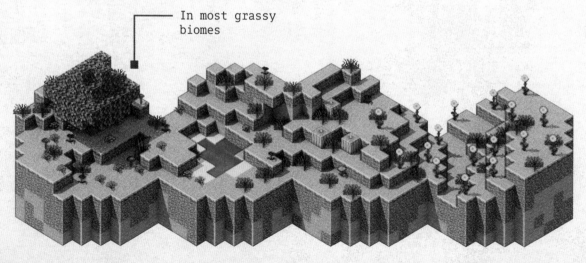

■ *A sheep that's spawned in a butcher villager's home. Er, best of luck, buddy!*

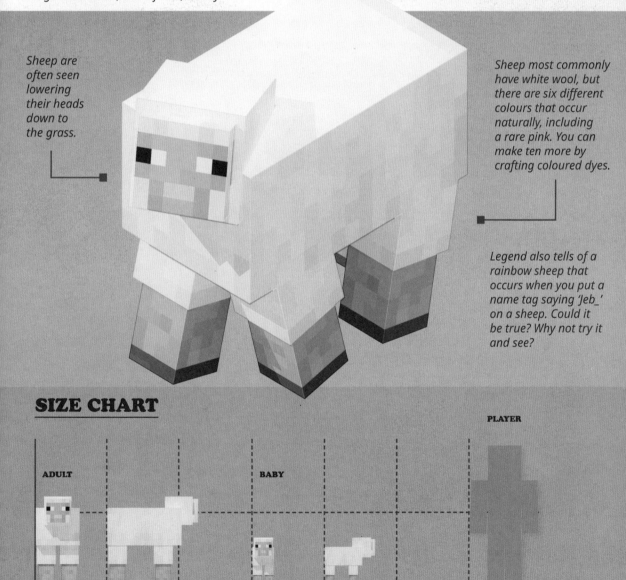

Sheep are often seen lowering their heads down to the grass.

Sheep most commonly have white wool, but there are six different colours that occur naturally, including a rare pink. You can make ten more by crafting coloured dyes.

Legend also tells of a rainbow sheep that occurs when you put a name tag saying 'Jeb_' on a sheep. Could it be true? Why not try it and see?

SIZE CHART

PLAYER

ADULT

BABY

HORSE

In an Overworld where we can happily ride pigs, is the horse really necessary? Absolutely! Horseback is one of the swiftest ways to travel. Horses can also help you jump higher AND you can equip them with armour. Just keep in mind that for such a 'passive' mob, they're not afraid to engage in some night-mare-ish behaviour ...

> *You will learn to love your horse, I am sure, but it might take some time before they trust you. I'm talking from experience! You see, horses aren't easily tamed. I've found that the best way to start is by feeding them, or going on a VERY short ride. I say short because they will rear and throw you off, which can be quite annoying. My horse had no interest in me, so I was rudely thrown off it so many times before we finally became besties. Now it's tame and lovely, and I've named it Sir Clip-Clop. Riding Sir Clip-Clop across the savanna at sunset is almost epic enough to make me forgive it for throwing me into the dirt blocks all those times!*

HABITAT

You'll find horses roaming around tucking into the grasses of the plains and savanna biomes. They are not as common as many other passive animal mobs, but they can be found in villages, where villagers always make sure they have hay in their pens.

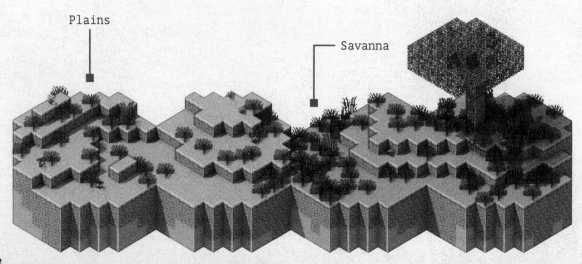

Plains

Savanna

18

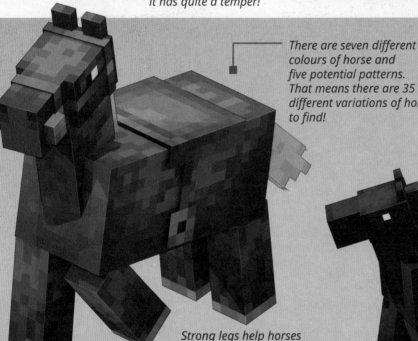

■ *This horse is rearing, showing it has quite a temper!*

There are seven different colours of horse and five potential patterns. That means there are 35 different variations of horse to find!

Horses can help you travel faster and will even leap up some slopes as you ride.

Strong legs help horses have high jump strength. The very strongest can leap above 5 blocks in height.

SIZE CHART

ADULT

BABY

PLAYER

WOLF

Acute, furry friend or a red-eyed monster? That all depends on your own treatment of the wolf. Ignore these grey beasts and they'll happily ignore you, too. Offer one a bone and you might just make a friend for life! Attack a wolf, however, and your life might just get a lot shorter ...

> *Why did I stay up all night fighting skeletons? To prove how tough I am, of course! Well, actually, I forgot to build a bed ... but on the plus side, I managed to get loads of bones for my trouble. I then kept offering wolves those bones until I finally tamed one. You've got a one-in-three chance of taming them with a bone, so just keep at it! Now I've got a cute companion which will help me in combat during my all-night skeleton fights. Superb news! Because I, er, may have forgotten to craft a bed again ...*

HABITAT

You'll find wolves in forests, taigas, groves, old growth taigas and snowy taigas. Don't forget that all wolves start off untamed, so you might want to collect some bones before you head off to explore those biomes.

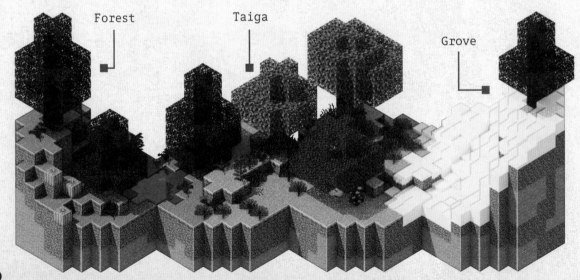

Forest

Taiga

Grove

■ *Skeletons are popular prey for the bone-loving wolf.*

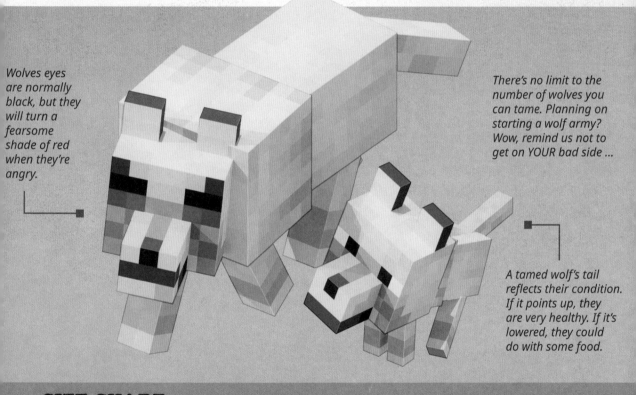

Wolves eyes are normally black, but they will turn a fearsome shade of red when they're angry.

There's no limit to the number of wolves you can tame. Planning on starting a wolf army? Wow, remind us not to get on YOUR bad side ...

A tamed wolf's tail reflects their condition. If it points up, they are very healthy. If it's lowered, they could do with some food.

SIZE CHART

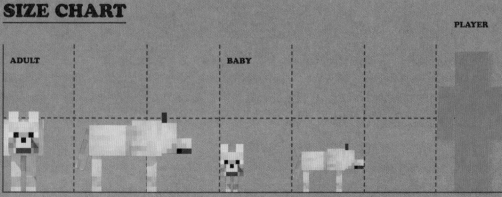

PLAYER

ADULT

BABY

SKELETON

Did you just hear the twang of a bowstring releasing an arrow? Then be warned that you could be in a skeleton's line of fire. These bony creatures love to practise archery on adventurers trying to survive their first night – or any other night. So come sundown, make sure you find shelter fast ... if you don't want this grim, grey mob to turn you into a target.

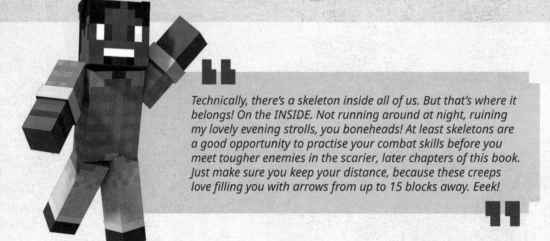

Technically, there's a skeleton inside all of us. But that's where it belongs! On the INSIDE. Not running around at night, ruining my lovely evening strolls, you boneheads! At least skeletons are a good opportunity to practise your combat skills before you meet tougher enemies in the scarier, later chapters of this book. Just make sure you keep your distance, because these creeps love filling you with arrows from up to 15 blocks away. Eeek!

HABITAT

The undead aren't picky, so with the exception of mushroom fields and the deep dark, skeletons spawn in low light in ALL Overworld biomes. Avoiding them while exploring is practically impossible. Make sure that you're properly prepared if you're venturing out in the dark of night, or into areas of low light, such as under trees and near cave openings.

Almost all
Overworld biomes

■ *Always find some cover. Skeletons are a surprisingly accurate shot!*

MOB NOTES

BEHAVIOUR: These hostile mobs will often catch you unaware and unprepared, so practise quickly equipping a shield.

DROPS: Skeletons sometimes drop arrows and bones, and even a skeleton skull if defeated by a charged creeper's explosion!

Most neutral and hostile mobs will ignore skeletons. But if one of the skeleton's fired arrows hits them, they'll attack it. Perhaps you could use this to your advantage?

Skeletons punish untidy explorers, happily picking up dropped weapons and armour, and equipping them to make themselves more deadly. Try not to leave weapons lying around.

Listen for the sounds of arrows landing nearby. If you hear one, move and take cover.

SIZE CHART

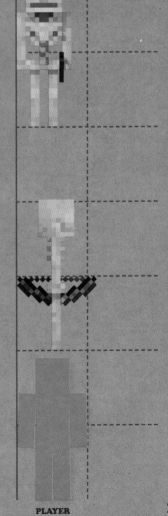

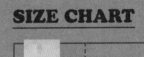

PLAYER

23

SPIDER

This creepiest of crawlies is a devastatingly fast mob, gleefully scuttling over blocks and walls to get you. You're safe so long as you encounter one in sunlight. But as soon as night falls ... you'd be wise not to underestimate these awesome arachnids.

Awww! This mob is so adorable. I just wanna hug them and run my fingers through their cute fur. Wait ... we're NOT talking about the rabbit? We're talking about the SPIDER?! This multi-legged monster isn't cute at all! It runs around on its eight legs, making light work of the Overworld's cumbersome cobwebs and giving off a general atmosphere of misery. Their ONLY redeeming feature is that spider eyes are a great ingredient for my potions.

HABITAT

With the exception of the mushroom fields and deep dark, spiders can spawn in all Overworld biomes. But the good news is that spiders are sometimes found on leaves, making them particularly common in forest biomes! Oh, that news is only 'good' if you love spiders, by the way. Sorry, I should have made that clear earlier.

Almost all
Overworld biomes

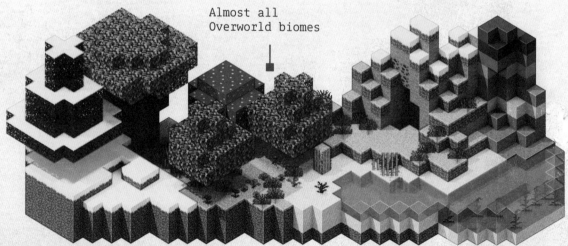

MOB NOTES

BEHAVIOUR: Don't get too comfortable near spiders in daylight. As soon as it gets dark, they'll go from friend to foe!
DROPS: As well as spider eyes, they will always drop string. You can use this to craft leads, fishing rods and bows.

■ *Walls are no match for a spider. Keep that in mind when trying to escape them!*

Spider eyes are colourful and glow in the dark, but they are a terrible choice of snack ...

Thanks to its eight legs, a spider can leap into attacks. The sound of one scurrying through caves is also one of the most sinister noises in the Overworld.

Spiders attack with their fangs, which deliver a nasty bite. Cave spider variants can also poison their victims with a single bite.

SIZE CHART

PLAYER

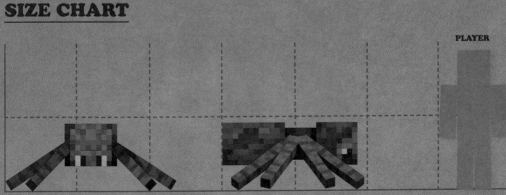

ZOMBIE

Can you hear groaning? It could be coming from you – when was the last time you ate? Even worse – it could be the deathly drone of a zombie! These monsters spend their lives shambling through the Overworld in search of fresh adventurers. Listen well for their telltale groan if you want to avoid a similar fate to theirs ...

> What could be more terrifying than a mob so evil that the only sound it makes is an otherworldly groan? Actually, even if it had a wonderful voice, you should still avoid the zombie! If you're good with a sword then one miserable flesh-muncher isn't too bad to deal with. But a group of these green-skinned ghouls can quickly overwhelm you. Be extra wary of the baby zombie! Its deceptive cuteness makes me wanna kneel down and pinch its cheek. I always forget it'll retaliate by punching mine. Hey!

HABITAT

Zombies spawn in every Overworld biome apart from the deep dark and mushroom fields. They are found in low light levels and will start to burn in direct sunlight, so you should be safe exploring during the day ... unless they're wearing a helmet to protect themselves. Groan!

Almost all
Overworld biomes

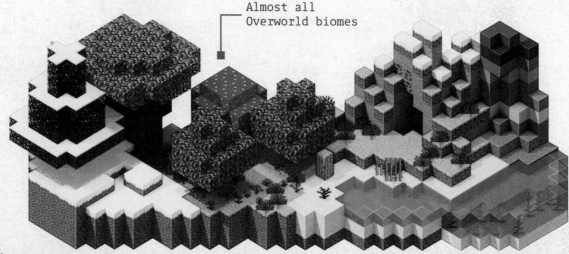

■ *You should be safe in there! Wait ... you DID remember to shut the door, right?*

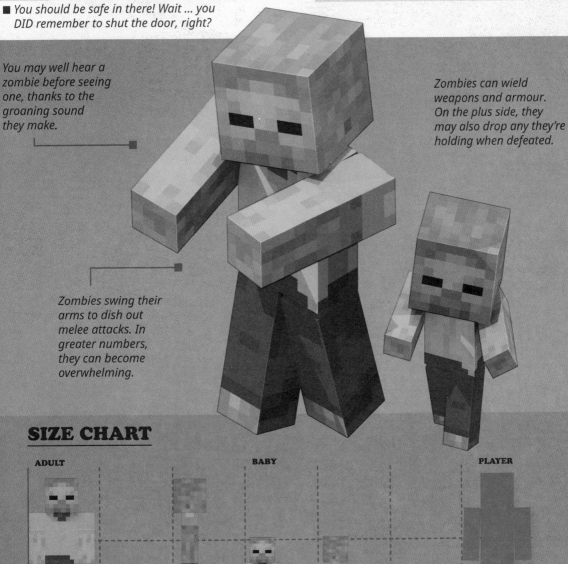

You may well hear a zombie before seeing one, thanks to the groaning sound they make.

Zombies can wield weapons and armour. On the plus side, they may also drop any they're holding when defeated.

Zombies swing their arms to dish out melee attacks. In greater numbers, they can become overwhelming.

SIZE CHART

ADULT

BABY

PLAYER

CREEPER

If you hear a HISS as you explore, rest assured that there are currently no snakes in the Overworld. That's the good news! The bad news is that the mob you ARE hearing, the creeper, is one of the deadliest. It's an explosive monster who will creep up on you and then go out with one heck of a bang!

The most famous mob in the entire Overworld is a green oblong that explodes if you go near it? Wow, the baby pig REALLY needs to fire its agent ... Look, you should never judge a book by its cover (wait, unless I am on the cover of a book. Then you should judge that, it's obviously brilliant!). However, when it's got 'creep' in the name, the facial expression of a total misery guts – explodey guts at that – and it's hissing and flashing, then MAYBE it's time for a nice run in the opposite direction? Hold up, you've already started running? Wait for me!

HABITAT

Creepers can be witnessed almost anywhere in the Overworld, with the exception of the deep dark and the mushroom fields. They can be surprisingly stealthy and good at creeping up on you. Wherever you are, always keep your ears open for their dreaded hissing sound!

Almost all
Overworld biomes

■ *We hope the photographer who took this was able to move away in time ...*

MOB NOTES

BEHAVIOUR: Creepers aren't afraid of much, but they stay well away from any ocelots and cats!

DROPS: Creepers can drop gunpowder, which can be used in some explosive crafting, such as TNT or firework rockets.

SIZE CHART

If you're within 16 blocks of a creeper, its head will turn towards you and it will begin to chase you.

If lightning strikes within four blocks of a creeper, it will become a charged creeper. Their explosions are almost twice as powerful.

A creeper's narrow and armless body will expand outwards when it prepares to explode.

EXPLORERS

Greetings, traveller. I'm Dwight Walker, the famous Overworld explorer! What's that? You've never heard of me? Ho, ho, ho! Good one. I'm so absurdly famous and admired, I honestly don't understand why they called it 'Minecraft' instead of 'Dwightcraft'. Anyway, I LOVE exploring! But be warned, my friend – the following pages contain increasingly dangerous mobs. Deadly mobs like ... the parrot. OK, that was a bad example. But be on your guard nonetheless, as there are plenty of hostile horrors incoming! Now, let us bravely turn the page together and meet these mobs. Er, can you go first? I'll, um, bravely protect us from behind. H-honest!

BEE

In charge of pollinating the Overworld's flowers and creating one of its sweetest treats, the bee is an essential part of Minecraft's ecosystem. With its bright yellow body and adorable antenna, many explorers have mistaken it for a fuzzy friend. But attempt to burgle the bee unprepared, and you'll soon discover it has a mighty sting in its tail ...

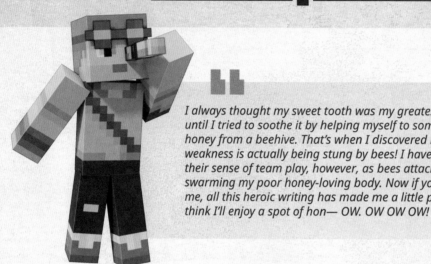

I always thought my sweet tooth was my greatest weakness, until I tried to soothe it by helping myself to some free honey from a beehive. That's when I discovered my greatest weakness is actually being stung by bees! I have to respect their sense of team play, however, as bees attack in a group, swarming my poor honey-loving body. Now if you'll excuse me, all this heroic writing has made me a little peckish, so I think I'll enjoy a spot of hon— OW. OW OW OW!

HABITAT

In the plains, sunflower plains and mangrove swamp, a small number of birch and oak trees have bee nests – as will cherry trees in cherry groves. They're even rarer in the various forest biomes. Keen beespotters will want to track down a meadow biome, where bees can almost certainly be found, along with bee nests on nearby birch and oak trees.

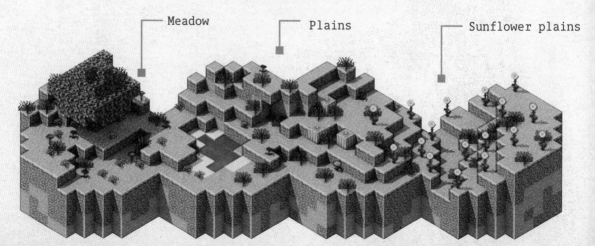

Meadow   Plains   Sunflower plains

MOB NOTES

BEHAVIOUR: Interestingly, bees appear to be diurnal, meaning they go home to their hive if it gets dark, or even rainy.

DID YOU KNOW?: Place a campfire under a bee nest and you can collect its honey without angering any bees.

■ Dwight once mistakenly thought he'd discovered the bee, and tried to name it 'The BumbleDwight'.

When a bee has collected pollen from a plant, you can see pollen spots on its back.

If you provoke a bee, it will become angered. Its eyes will turn red and it will swarm after you with the entire hive.

Bees will take pollen from flowers, such as azalea and mangrove saplings. They use this to pollinate many crops, such as wheat, potatoes and carrots, making them grow faster.

SIZE CHART

PLAYER

ADULT

BABY

DONKEY

Have you ever wished for a horse with longer ears, darker ankles and a mane that doesn't stick out as much? Thankfully, the donkey is here to make those very specific dreams come true. This magnificent mare is an excellent travelling companion because it is capable of carrying both you and a chest. Imagine how many more items you can take with you!

I simply love taking in the wonders of the Overworld on the back of a tamed donkey. Because when you're carrying as many essential exploring tools as I am, you need a steed capable of carrying a chest! What's that? You searched my chest and found that my 'exploring tools' were 960 cakes? Well, er, you see ... it's important not to explore on an e-empty stomach! Donkey, get us out of here NOW. The readers are asking too many awkward questions again ...

HABITAT

Donkeys roam in the plains, sunflower plains, savanna and meadow biomes. The plains are one of the Overworld's most common biomes, so you hopefully won't have to search for very long before you find a delightful donkey companion.

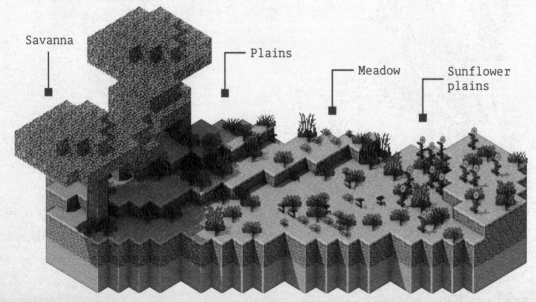

Savanna — Plains — Meadow — Sunflower plains

It's easy to see why donkeys like the sunflower plains. It's one of the Overworld's prettiest biomes!

MOB NOTES

BEHAVIOURS: They won't enjoy you trying to saddle them if they're untamed. Seriously, tame them first!

DROPS: Defeated donkeys may drop leather, and any saddles or chests they were equipped with – including the chest contents.

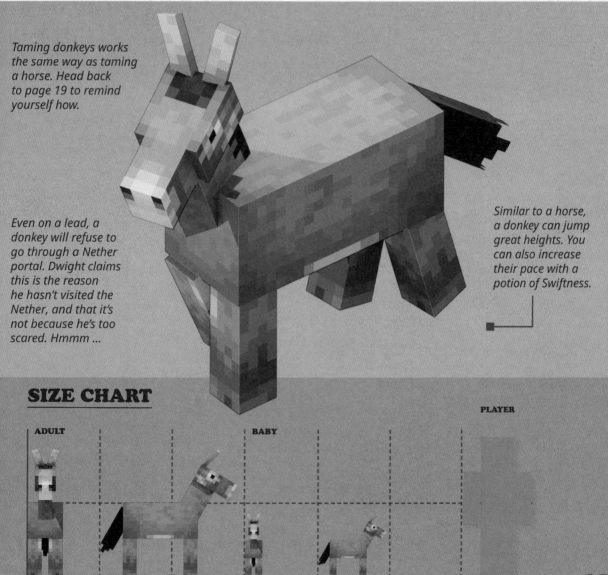

Taming donkeys works the same way as taming a horse. Head back to page 19 to remind yourself how.

Even on a lead, a donkey will refuse to go through a Nether portal. Dwight claims this is the reason he hasn't visited the Nether, and that it's not because he's too scared. Hmmm …

Similar to a horse, a donkey can jump great heights. You can also increase their pace with a potion of Swiftness.

SIZE CHART

ADULT

BABY

PLAYER

MULE

he reddish-brown offspring of a horse and a donkey, the mule is yet another fine choice of transport for an explorer. Closer in size to the horse, but with similar ears, coat and mane to a donkey, the mule is essentially the best of both mobs. Its parents must be so proud!

Why are there so many rideable mobs in my section of the book? Are they trying to imply I'm lazy? How dare they! I'd get down from my mule and challenge them to fisticuffs at dawn for that, if I could be bothered. Anyway, the mule is my favourite of all the Overworld's equine mobs. I just love the colour of its coat. It's just a terrible shame that the mule can't breed, so there is no way I can fulfil my dream of starting 'Dwight's Mule Farm'. But there's nothing stopping me from breeding plenty of horses and donkeys and then getting many more mules, I guess!

HABITAT

Mules are one of the rare mobs that aren't found naturally, and there's only one way you can get one. You'll need to find both a donkey and a horse first. Once you do, you'll need to feed them a golden apple or a golden carrot to get them to breed. Sorry, they don't come cheap – but before you know it, you'll have your own mule!

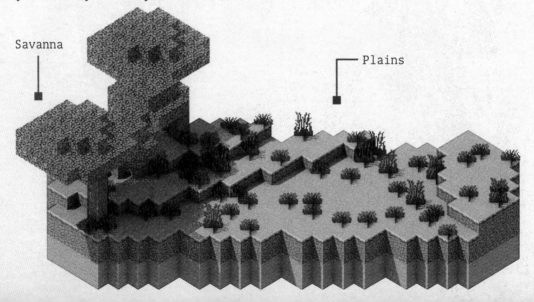

Savanna

Plains

■ *You'll have to matchmake a horse and a donkey if you want to get a mule!*

MOB NOTES

BEHAVIOUR: Every time you walk near this mob, it will turn its head to stare at you. How inquisitive!

DROPS: A defeated mule will drop leather. If it was equipped with a saddle or a chest, it will drop those, too – plus any items that were stored in the chest.

You can attach a lead to a mule and it won't try to stop you.

A baby mule takes 20 minutes to reach adulthood. Can't wait that long? It'll grow up faster if fed sugar, wheat, apples, golden apples, golden carrots or hay bales!

These rideable mobs can slowly regenerate their own health. How rare!

SIZE CHART

ADULT

BABY

PLAYER

CAMEL

A mob that understands the greatest journeys in the Overworld are the ones we embark on together, the camel allows two adventurers to ride it simultaneously. Those tired of having their mood darkened by the miserable face of the creeper should seek out a camel – its oh-so-satisfied smirk is incredibly infectious!

A mob built for two? Ha! Dwight Walker has no need of a sidekick! Or any friends. That's, er, the only reason I travel alone! Still, I'll admit that the desolate deserts aren't quite as lonely now I have this smiling camel carrying me along. I also can't help admiring a mob that knows to regularly treat itself to a nice sit-down. Now I just need to make a friend to ride one with me ... wait, I wasn't meant to admit that in the book. Editor, delete that last sentence immediately! Also, why won't you respond to my invitations to go camel riding?

HABITAT

Somewhat unsurprisingly, you'll find camels in the desert biome, specifically in any villages you find there. Be warned that if a camel is defeated, another one won't show up in the village. But you would never do something as dreadful as defeat a camel ... would you?

Desert village

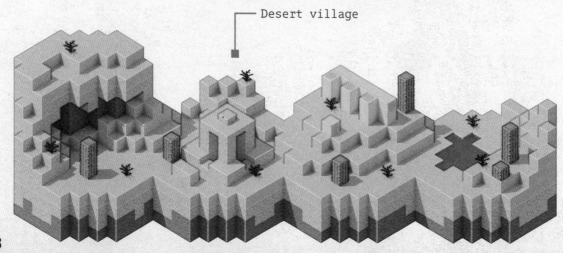

■ *Sadly there's no way to thank a camel by carrying IT through the desert. Hardly seems fair ...*

MOB NOTES

OBSERVATIONS: They might be slow but camels can carry two of you, and will gain speed when travelling across flat terrain.
DID YOU KNOW?: Camels often sit down to take a break from the desert heat. When they do, they won't follow you – even if you're offering up some cactus!

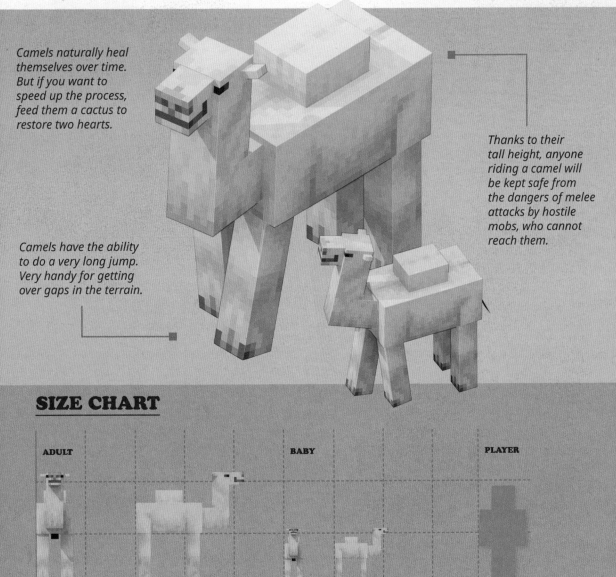

Camels naturally heal themselves over time. But if you want to speed up the process, feed them a cactus to restore two hearts.

Thanks to their tall height, anyone riding a camel will be kept safe from the dangers of melee attacks by hostile mobs, who cannot reach them.

Camels have the ability to do a very long jump. Very handy for getting over gaps in the terrain.

SIZE CHART

ADULT

BABY

PLAYER

SNIFFER

Once thought to be a long lost and extinct species, the sniffer had been absent for so long that many natural history buffs considered it a myth. Now, this ancient mob is back and ready to waddle its way across the Overworld, one loud sniff at time. Baby snifflets grow up into huge mobs that will uncover ancient seeds. Plant these and they could grow into unique and colourful decorative plants.

■

> *Finding a sniffer is no easy feat, and I should know. They are found only by experts. Er, well, the truth is, I encountered one thanks to Riley Waverider, who you'll meet later! They had been diving around a warm ocean ruins and found eggs nestled in some suspicious sand, which they gave to me. The eggs were like nothing I had seen before, so I stayed with them day and night until they hatched. When they did, I found myself face-to-face with a mob I didn't recognise. It soon began aimlessly wandering, as if hunting for something. When it found some torchflower seeds, I kept them safe as they can be used to heal an injured sniffer.*

HABITAT

You can only find sniffer eggs in suspicious sand, specifically suspicious sand found in ocean ruins of warm ocean biomes. Once they hatch, you can lead them anywhere you choose. As adults, they can dig for seeds in dirt, grass blocks, podzol, coarse dirt, rooted dirt, moss blocks, mud and muddy mangrove roots.

Warm ocean

A sniffer tracking seeds underground.

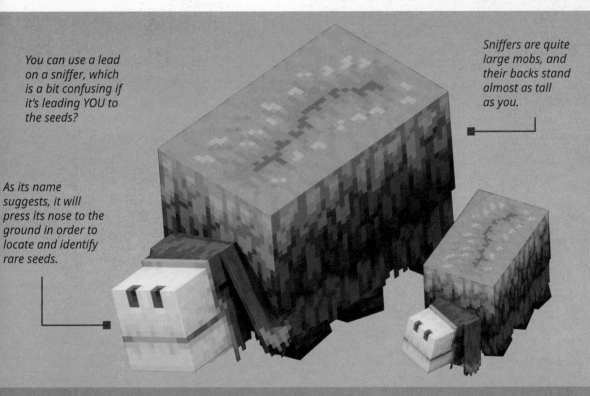

You can use a lead on a sniffer, which is a bit confusing if it's leading YOU to the seeds?

Sniffers are quite large mobs, and their backs stand almost as tall as you.

As its name suggests, it will press its nose to the ground in order to locate and identify rare seeds.

SIZE CHART

ADULT   BABY   PLAYER

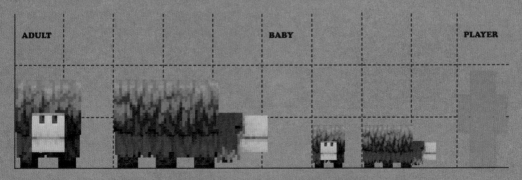

41

PARROT

Hiss! Groan! Squawk! Few mobs have as vast a dynamic vocal range as the parrot. This brightly feathered rascal is quite the mimic, capable of impersonating other mobs. Are they a helpful warning of unseen dangers, or an unwanted source of free panic attacks?

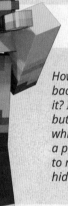

> How come none of the parrots I've met on my travels ever repeat back 'Dwight Walker is the best!', no matter how many times I say it? I thought I heard one say 'Dwight should consider showering', but that was probably just because I haven't washed my ears in a while. Anyway, I adore these brightly coloured birds! Even though a parrot can trick you into thinking a spider is nearby, causing you to run home weeping and spend the rest of the week sobbing and hiding under the bed. Er, a hypothetical example.

HABITAT

You'll find parrots flying around in the various jungle biomes. They're fairly rare, though, so keep your eyes peeled for a burst of bright colour amongst all that green!

Jungle biomes

■ *Parrots come in five different colours. Can you discover them all?*

MOB NOTES

BEHAVIOUR: Parrots seem to enjoy being impersonators of other mobs. Either that or they enjoy giving you quite a fright when you think a creeper is approaching! They have somewhat of a bad reaction to cocoa. How bad? Feeding them a cookie is fatal!
DROPS: Defeated parrots drop 1–2 feathers.

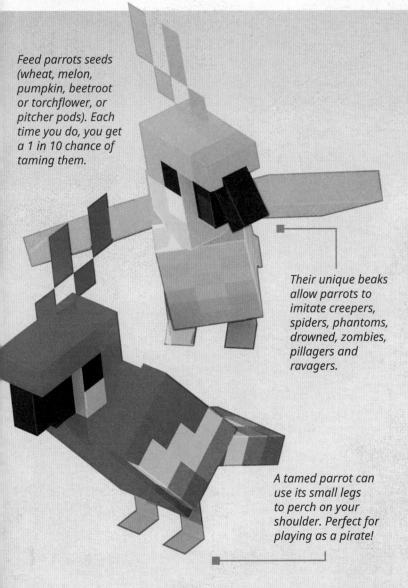

Feed parrots seeds (wheat, melon, pumpkin, beetroot or torchflower, or pitcher pods). Each time you do, you get a 1 in 10 chance of taming them.

Their unique beaks allow parrots to imitate creepers, spiders, phantoms, drowned, zombies, pillagers and ravagers.

A tamed parrot can use its small legs to perch on your shoulder. Perfect for playing as a pirate!

SIZE CHART

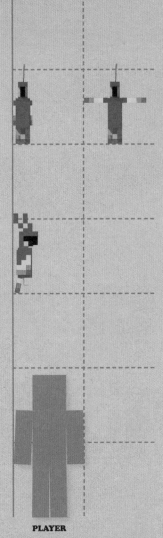

PLAYER

43

GOAT

Now, here we have a mob that truly values the high life. The goat loves to ascend mountain peaks and it is well worth pursuing, as it offers both goat horns and milk. Just be warned that they like to ram unsuspecting targets within 16 blocks of them, and that some of them possess quite a scream ...

I got called a GOAT once. Greatest of all Time! But disappointingly, I soon realised they meant the animal kind of goat, because of my habit of screaming quite a lot. Bah! The joke is on them, because I'm proud to be associated with this fine mountain-dwelling mob! I love goats and I can tell it's mutual. Why else would this goat right here be lowering its head (out of respect), stomping its foot (in admiration) and running towards me (presumably for a hug)? OK, slow down now, Mr Goat, you don't want to accidentally ram me off this mount—ARGHHHHHHHH!

HABITAT

Goats are fond of mountain biomes and are often found navigating the steep hills of colder mountain areas. You might need to be good with heights if you want to meet one – and make sure you pack supplies.

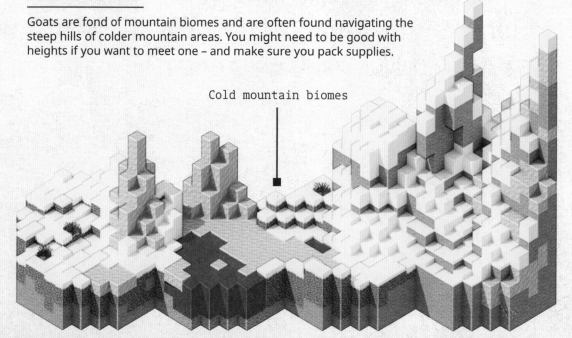

Cold mountain biomes

■ *What happened to the adventurer who was meant to be in this photo? Hope they didn't get rammed ...*

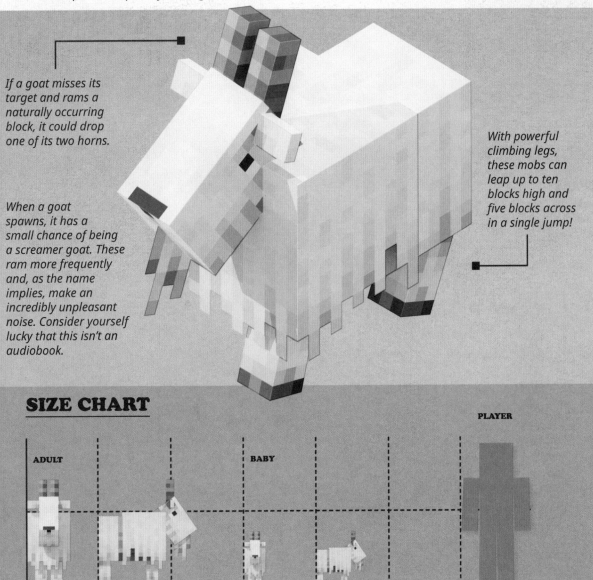

If a goat misses its target and rams a naturally occurring block, it could drop one of its two horns.

When a goat spawns, it has a small chance of being a screamer goat. These ram more frequently and, as the name implies, make an incredibly unpleasant noise. Consider yourself lucky that this isn't an audiobook.

With powerful climbing legs, these mobs can leap up to ten blocks high and five blocks across in a single jump!

SIZE CHART

PLAYER

ADULT

BABY

OCELOT

A spotted jungle animal that's ironically quite hard to spot. Most likely because the ocelot would rather sneak up on you, especially if you're a chicken or a baby turtle. You'll need to be holding something fishy if you want to win over this carnivorous cat!

I've spent years thoroughly exploring every inch of the Overworld's jungles. OK, fine, that's mainly because I can't find my way out ... but I did spot this adorable kitty-cat! 'Awww!' I bravely roared upon discovering the ocelot. Luckily, I hadn't eaten my raw salmon and cod I'd been saving for lunch, so I offered it to the ocelot instead. Every time you feed it, you have a chance of taming it! Soon I was the proud owner of my new ocelot, Mr PrettyKitty (categorically the best cat name ever). Who needs to know how to escape the jungle when I have such a lovely pet now? Um, me. I need to know. Please tell me.

HABITAT

They are rare, but ocelots can be found in all the jungle biomes and meadows. You could try to draw them out by using chickens or baby turtles as bait (you meanie!). If you discover one, move with caution – if you move your head too quickly, this cat will flee from you.

Jungle biomes

Meadow

■ *Huh? Where's the ocelot? Drat, it's hard to get a photo of one when they're so fast!*

Creepers and phantoms like to keep their distance from the ocelot, so keeping a tamed one by your side is a great way to ward off those potential threats.

Ocelots are immune to fall damage, so feel free to throw them off cliffs. Actually, please don't do that.

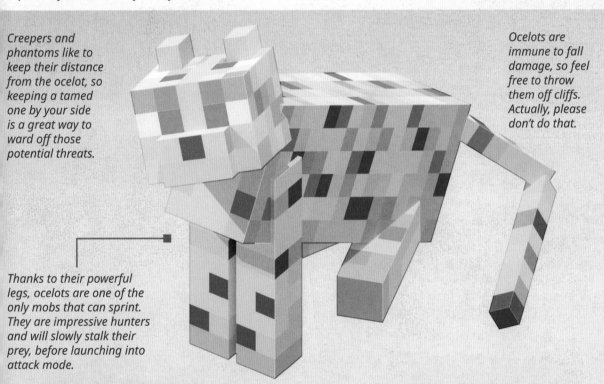

Thanks to their powerful legs, ocelots are one of the only mobs that can sprint. They are impressive hunters and will slowly stalk their prey, before launching into attack mode.

SIZE CHART

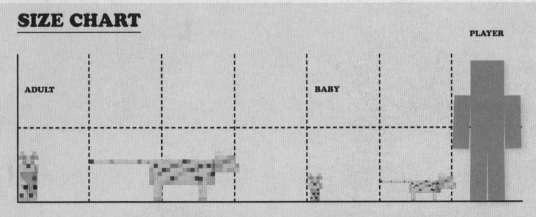

ADULT   BABY   PLAYER

RABBIT

A strong contender for the Overworld's most adorable mob, until you discover what they've done to your carrot collection. The rabbit hops happily about. Then it hops with far more fear, once it realises it's in the vicinity of a hostile mob. It should probably avoid you, too, if you're looking for rabbit hide, raw rabbit or a rabbit's foot!

> *Chasing these cute little mobs all across the Overworld has exhausted even me! I've had to visit flower forests, taigas and meadows to track down the brown, black and salt-and-pepper rabbits. Then I had to wrap up warm and investigate the snowy taigas, snowy plains, snowy slopes and groves to find white and black-and-white rabbits. After all that, I was too cold and shattered to seek out a golden rabbit in a desert biome, and I've exhausted my carrot supplies. Anybody got any leftover carrots? Dwight needs energy, sharp-ish!*

HABITAT

There are many different colours of rabbits and they can be found in many of the Overworld's biomes. They are quite rare, so if you really need to find one, the most common variant is the golden rabbit, which can be located in desert biomes.

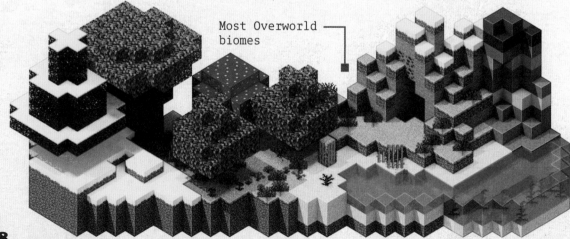

Most Overworld biomes

MOB NOTES

OBSERVATIONS: Rabbits are usually found on their own, making them an even harder mob to spot.

DROPS: You can expect defeated rabbits to drop rabbit hide, which can be used to craft leather. They could also drop raw rabbit and a rabbit's foot.

■ *Rabbits will leap off cliffs in pursuit of carrots. Yes, they are a tasty snack, but please be careful, rabbits!*

There is a 95% chance a baby rabbit will inherit the same fur as their parents. However, there is a 5% chance their fur type will match the biome it spawns in.

Try naming a rabbit 'Toast' using a name tag and then see what happens ...

There's a small chance a defeated rabbit will drop a rabbit's foot; a crucial component if you want to brew a potion of Leaping.

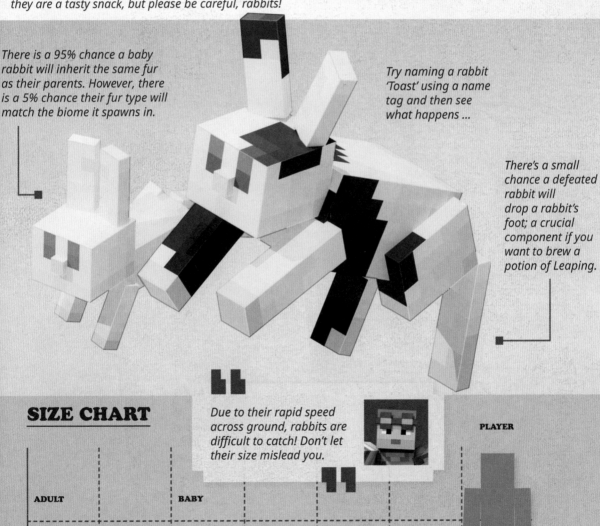

SIZE CHART

Due to their rapid speed across ground, rabbits are difficult to catch! Don't let their size mislead you.

PLAYER

ADULT

BABY

49

MOOSHROOM

A bizarre cow that can pull off red AND being covered in mushrooms? That's a tricky fashion combo for even the most experienced of models. The mooshroom is a pun-tacular choice for any farmer considering moving into the vegetarian market. Perfect for those looking for a mob that both moos and makes stews!

Exploring certainly does build up an appetite! Especially if, like me, you forgot to pack any food. Blast! Luckily, I'm quite the flower collector and stumbled across a brown mooshroom. Such a rare sight! Did you know that if you feed a brown mooshroom certain flowers before milking them, you'll get a bowl of suspicious stew? The effects of the stew upon your body will depend entirely on the flower! Feed the mooshroom a poppy and the stew will give you Night Vision. Try an oxeye daisy and you'll get health regeneration! Feed it the lily of the valley and the stew I just ate will— urk! Oh dear, suddenly I don't feel so good ...

HABITAT

The only place you can find a mooshroom is the rare mushroom fields biome. Therefore, if you're lucky enough to chance upon them, it's a good idea to breed them. Feed them plenty of wheat and you'll soon have more mooshrooms!

Mushroom Fields

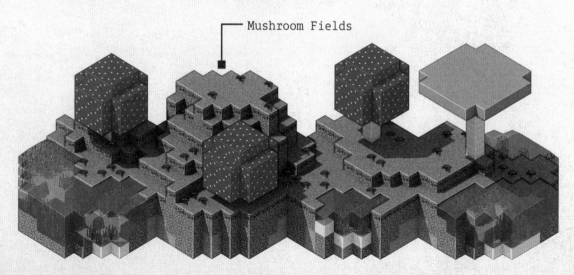

MOB NOTES

OBSERVATIONS: Although this is an incredibly rare mob, found only in the mushroom fields, they can be found in herds of up to eight mooshrooms.

DROPS: Any defeated mooshroom may drop leather and raw beef – which will be steak if it was defeated while on fire!

■ It's safer to enjoy this photo rather than braving a thunderstorm to see a mooshroom turn brown.

If a red mooshroom is struck by lightning, it'll transform into a brown mooshroom. And vice versa, if a brown one is struck!

If you shear a mooshroom, you'll get five mushrooms. But be warned that this will turn your mooshroom into a regular cow.

SIZE CHART

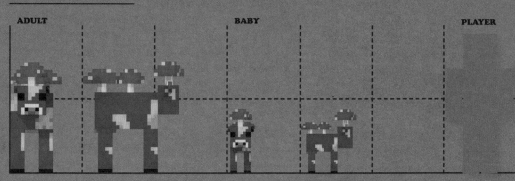

ADULT   BABY   PLAYER

PANDA

Quite possibly the Overworld's most emotional mob, the panda gets away with being so dramatic thanks to its adorable appearance (making sneezing look cute is no easy feat). These furry bamboo fiends might just be my favourite Minecraft mob. Sure, they're hard to find – but the hours of searching are more than worth the wait. That's a Dwight promise!

■

> *On my travels, I've encountered every kind of panda. Worried pandas have a fearful expression, particularly during thunderstorms. Normal pandas frown at me, even though I'm lovely. Playful pandas stick their tongues out at me, even though, as I just said, I'M LOVELY. Aggressive pandas take it personally when I accidentally tickle them. Weak baby pandas are often sneezy, something I sadly learnt while examining them close-up. Lazy pandas move extra slowly, which makes them the slowest mobs in the Overworld. They've inspired me to become lazier myself! So lazy, in fact, that I'm not even going to bother finishing this sentence properl ...*

HABITAT

You'll find pandas in jungle biomes, but be warned that they are quite rare. Even in the bamboo jungles, where they're most common, it is still incredibly rare to see them. Crossing paths with all the different panda types will take a lot of effort!

Jungle

Bamboo Jungle

OBSERVATIONS: Pandas are the only mob that can have different personalities. Which will you encounter? If there is a thunderstorm, a worried panda will start shaking and will attempt to hide its face with its paws. Aw, don't be scared!

DROPS: Defeated pandas will drop bamboo.

■ *Everyone knows pandas enjoy bamboo, but they also have a weakness for cake. Relatable!*

They may not look athletic, but playful pandas love jumping and rolling over – even if it means accidentally falling from high places and receiving damage.

On very rare occasions, pandas have been known to spawn with zombie variant jockeys riding their backs.

Pandas most often come in black and white, but there's a brown-and-white variant out there, too.

SIZE CHART

PLAYER

ADULT

BABY

PHANTOM

Having trouble sticking to a regular bedtime? Meet the Overworld's most terrifying incentive for getting a good night's rest. The phantom, also known as the monster of the night skies, appears if you don't go to sleep for three days. We'd highly recommend bashing a bed together and getting under the covers before it swoops down to introduce itself ...

> *My friends are GREAT at falling asleep, particularly when I'm telling them stories of my adventures, but I've never been very good at going to bed. Unfortunately, that means I've had many a midnight skirmish with a phantom. A fearsome opponent indeed, this mob can take off six hearts in a single blow! Meanwhile my courageous counterattacks usually aren't quick enough to cause damage ... unless I accidentally hit myself in the face. Look, give me a break, here. I haven't slept in days!*

HABITAT

The phantom seems unbothered by the differing climates of various biomes and has been spotted all across the Overworld. As it only appears at night or during a thunderstorm, it's possible that it slinks out from any number of locations. However, it will only spawn if you're out in the open and not taking cover under a light-obscuring block.

All Overworld biomes

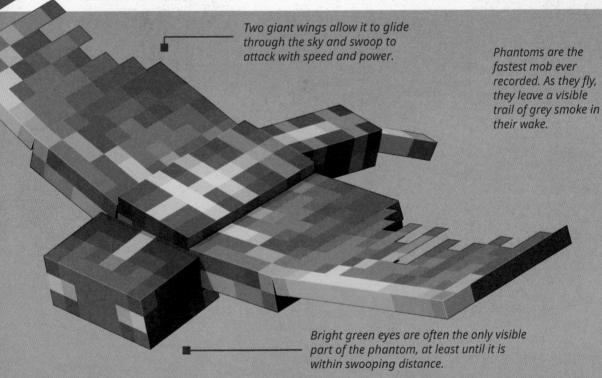

MOB NOTES

OBSERVATIONS: Phantoms will stay away from ocelots, so if you're not getting enough sleep, at least keep a kitty nearby.
DID YOU KNOW?: When defeated it might drop a phantom membrane. This can be used to brew a potion of Slow Falling, making you temporarily immune to fall damage.

■ *Oh dear. Looks like this adventurer decided to build a bed a little too late ...*

Two giant wings allow it to glide through the sky and swoop to attack with speed and power.

Phantoms are the fastest mob ever recorded. As they fly, they leave a visible trail of grey smoke in their wake.

Bright green eyes are often the only visible part of the phantom, at least until it is within swooping distance.

SIZE CHART

PLAYER

CHICKEN JOCKEY

Baby creatures are cute. Chickens are cute. Surely a combination of the two should be doubly adorable? No, sadly, the chicken jockey is more ARGH-dorable. Charming chickens become foul fowls once you stick a baby husk, baby zombie, baby zombie villager, baby zombified piglin or a baby drowned on their backs. What did this poor poultry do to deserve becoming the transport option of choice for some of the Overworld's most creepy kids?

One of the things I've learnt on my travels is that I can't ride chickens. You don't need to know how I found that out – it's far more vital that I inform you of the dangers of chicken jockeys! Baby versions of hostile mobs, moving around on the backs of chickens, are not to be underestimated. They behave a lot like zombies, so one or two can be dealt with fairly easily, but any number above that should have you strategically running away screaming. Is this karma for all the delicious chicken I've consumed over the years? I hope not, because I'm starved, and could really go for some now actually ...

HABITAT

Baby zombies and their variants can appear in almost all Overworld biomes, so if they're sharing a biome with a chicken there's a chance they'll become a chicken jockey. Chicken jockeys can also spawn in biomes where chickens won't on their own, such as deserts.

Almost all
Overworld biomes

MOB NOTES

OBSERVATIONS: Despite his best efforts, Dwight has been unable to mount and ride a chicken himself.

DID YOU KNOW?: Defeating a chicken jockey will cause the riding mob and the chicken to each have seperate drops, plus a healthy dose of experience!

■ *Don't be fooled by its cute appearance – this combo is nothing but bad news!*

Despite the chicken doing all the work, a chicken jockey will only travel where the baby hostile mob wishes to go, especially if it wishes to attack you!

SIZE CHART

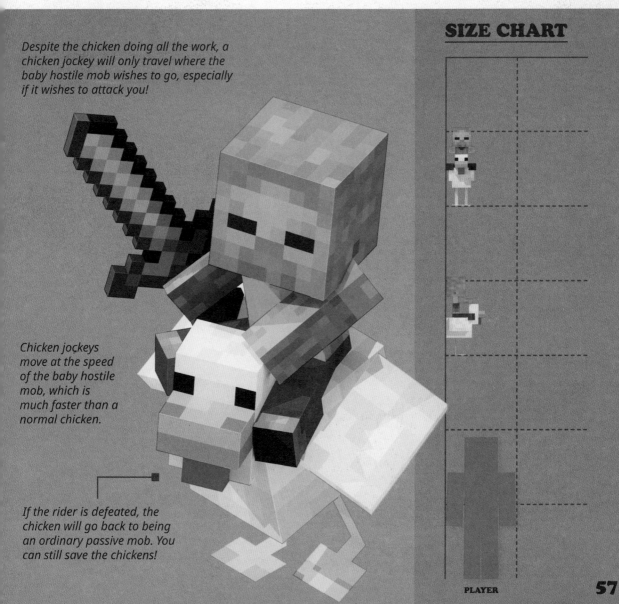

Chicken jockeys move at the speed of the baby hostile mob, which is much faster than a normal chicken.

If the rider is defeated, the chicken will go back to being an ordinary passive mob. You can still save the chickens!

SKELETON HORSE
& SKELETON HORSEMAN

You spot a horse in the plains but something looks off about it. That's probably just because it's hard to see during a thunderstorm, right? Wrong. Because once you get within ten blocks of a skeleton horse, lightning strikes, and now you have four skeleton horsemen to deal with! The skeleton horsemen are so sinister that I almost can't write about them without wanting to go and take cover somewhere safe!

> *Look, despite their looks, there's nothing wrong with skeleton horses on their own – apart from being a bit of a bony ride. But if you see a skeleton horse alone during a storm, it could be a trap. Step too close to a skeleton horse and a lightning strike will summon not one, but four skeleton horsemen. Yes, four. I'd usually say something typically brave and insightful here, but this mob's so horrid, I really don't have the words!*

HABITAT

Wherever you are in the Overworld, there is a small chance that a skeleton horse will spawn, when lightning strikes during a storm. Get too close, and it will be replaced by four horses ridden by skeletons. Defeat any of the riders and their skeleton horse will remain – and it will be tame.

All Overworld biomes

■ *The electrifying process of a skeleton horse gaining a horseman!*

MOB NOTES

OBSERVATIONS: Don't get excited about feeding your tamed skeleton horse. They do not – and will not – eat!

DID YOU KNOW?: Even though the skeleton horse itself is neutral, its rider will be hostile towards you. It can survive in daylight thanks to its helmet. Agh!

Each skeleton horseman spawns with an enchanted bow and enchanted helmet, so try to pick one up if you manage to defeat one.

If you defeat the horseman, the skeleton horse itself will be passive and tamed – but you'll still need a saddle to ride it!

Skeleton horses are one of the fastest running mobs in the Overworld. You can even ride them underwater. An undead horse doesn't need to breathe ... but you still will.

SIZE CHART

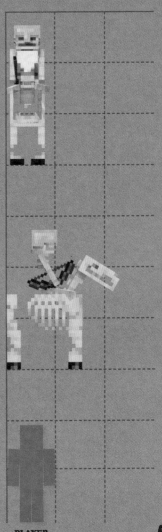

PLAYER

59

SPIDER JOCKEY

Encountering a spider or cave spider is already a scary situation. So the presence of a spider jockey is nothing short of a nightmare. Their rider can be a skeleton, a stray or a Wither skeleton – three hostile mobs that were already threatening, without the sinister scuttling advantages that riding a spider offers. For anyone scared of spiders, read on to get a better idea of how these are even scarier ... Sorry, this can't be easy to read!

> *At least chicken jockeys are half cute! A hostile mob on top of a spider is bad news on top of more bad news. Like the time I was bitten by a spider and fell backwards into a cobweb. Spiders can get very close to you, very quickly, and climbing walls is no challenge for them. The spider jockey sadly has those perks, plus a hostile rider, so it is double trouble if you see one of them coming your way. I even once witnessed a baby zombie hop on to a spider to become a spider jockey. Groan! It isn't all bad news, though. My work here is nearly done, so I can finally stop pretending I'm brave and steer clear of mobs such as this.*

HABITAT

Apart from the mushroom fields and deep dark, spiders spawn in all Overworld biomes. Sometimes, they will spawn as spider jockeys with another mob riding them. If you're adventuring in any snowy biomes, there's a small chance a spider will spawn with a stray on its back.

Almost all
Overworld biomes

MOB NOTES

OBSERVATIONS: A skeleton and a spider jockey will turn on each other if they accidentally damage one another. Leave them to it and plan your escape!

DID YOU KNOW?: Defeat a spider jockey and the skeleton and its rider will drop their own individual items.

■ How did the skeleton climb the wall? Quickly, and on a spider. That's how!

Hostile mobs riding spiders retain all their abilities and dangers, making meeting one a particularly petrifying experience.

Spiders can climb walls, which means the hostile mobs atop a spider jockey now have a new advantage. If hiding out of sight was how you avoided skeleton archers, think again!

Thankfully, spider jockeys have a very small chance of spawning. They're one of the rarest mobs in this whole book!

SIZE CHART

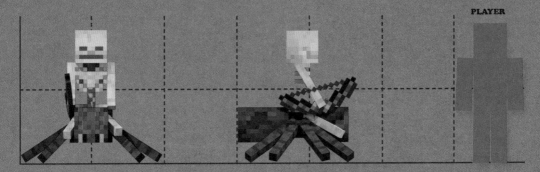

PLAYER

VILLAGES

Hrrrm! Hrrrm? Hrrm hrrm! Oh, I'm sorry – I've been trying to talk like villagers but haven't quite figured it out! I'm Dr Dora Settlewell and it's a pleasure to welcome you to my section of this book. I'm something of an obsessive when it comes to the villages of the Overworld. I travel between villages, trading with the locals, admiring their homes and politely asking if there's somewhere I can cower and hide during illager raids. I must say, villager hosts are usually most accommodating!

Oh, yes, I should probably warn you that this section isn't all merriment and polite hrrrm-ing! Pillagers, illagers and other no-good-at-all-agers are found in these areas. I feel it's my duty to catalogue them comprehensively and warn you about them, too! Now, have you got everything you need? Splendid! In which case, let's get going!

VILLAGER

After fighting creepers, skeletons and a sneaking suspicion that the Overworld doesn't want you here, it's nice to stumble upon a village and meet a friendly face. While villagers are a chatty bunch who enjoy exchanging information, you won't be able to understand them. Their delightful villages are welcoming places to visit, unless they're in the holds of a raid ...

> *I must say, I am a big fan of trading with villagers. It can be a very rewarding activity, so I always make sure I am stocked up on emeralds whenever I visit somewhere new. They often have all sorts of useful items to trade! Of course, trading alone isn't why I love visiting villages – they are a useful place to stop off for several reasons, mostly to find a safe bed to sleep in. Oh ok, and to borrow some items from their chests. I'm assuming their cries of 'hrrm' mean 'go right ahead!' Sadly, being a villager researcher doesn't pay too well, so I've had to, ahem, 'borrow' a fair few resources from their villages. I'm sure they don't mind ...*

HABITAT

Villages can naturally spawn in plains, sunflower plains, snowy plains, snowy taiga, savanna, taiga, meadows and desert biomes. Villagers are instantly recognisable, but their appearances change depending on what biome they are in and what their occupations are.

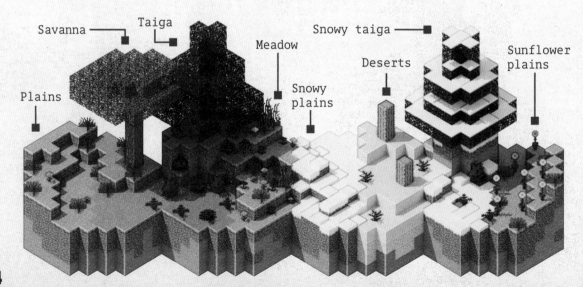

■ These villagers have entered love mode. Awww!

OBSERVATIONS: Be on high alert in stormy weather. If a poor villager is unfortunate enough to be hit by lightning, it will mysteriously be replaced by a witch.
DID YOU KNOW?: If you defeat a village raid, baby villagers may offer you gifts of poppies or wheat seeds.

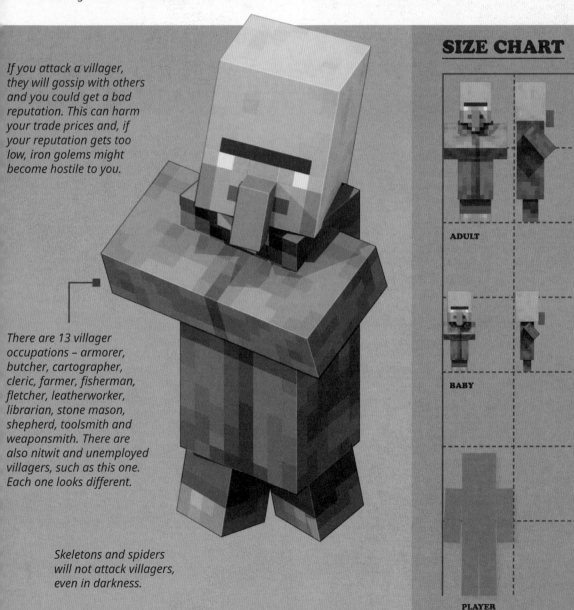

If you attack a villager, they will gossip with others and you could get a bad reputation. This can harm your trade prices and, if your reputation gets too low, iron golems might become hostile to you.

There are 13 villager occupations – armorer, butcher, cartographer, cleric, farmer, fisherman, fletcher, leatherworker, librarian, stone mason, shepherd, toolsmith and weaponsmith. There are also nitwit and unemployed villagers, such as this one. Each one looks different.

Skeletons and spiders will not attack villagers, even in darkness.

SIZE CHART

ADULT

BABY

PLAYER

CAT

Did you know that villages are an excellent source of cats? But these feisty felines won't necessarily remain in their home villages. These strays prefer to stray, exploring the Overworld, and will approach anyone holding cod or salmon. Tame one, and you'll have yourself a cute companion and a surprisingly excellent bodyguard from phantoms and creepers.

> As a professional village researcher, I need to keep a level head and not be cuted out by any mobs. But look what I'm up against here! Add an 'e' on the end and the word 'cat' is practically the word 'cute' – only slightly misspelt! These fantastic felines make excellent pets, and their soft meows break up the endless hrrrm-ing I usually endure in these villages (er, not that I'm complaining, villagers. Please don't kick me out). Having an inventory full of fish may risk making you the smelliest explorer in the entire Overworld. Personally, I think that's a risk worth taking, so you're always ready to offer a cat a tasty treat. Oh, I can't hold back anymore – this mob is basically purrfect!

HABITAT

They frequently spawn in villages, but swamp huts in the swamp biome are also a good source of cats, albeit a slightly more risky one. Black cats spawn in these huts, but they are also home to witches – so if you're going to risk tracking one down, be prepared to defend yourself!

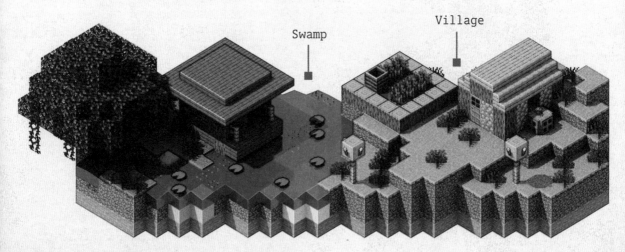

Swamp

Village

OBSERVATIONS: Somewhat surprisingly, creepers and phantoms – two mighty and feared mobs – seem to be afraid of cats. Keeping a tamed cat close by is a good plan.
DID YOU KNOW?: In every Overworld village, you can find one cat for every four owned beds. So cute!

■ *Maybe if we ask nicely, the witch will give us their cat? Er, you go first ...*

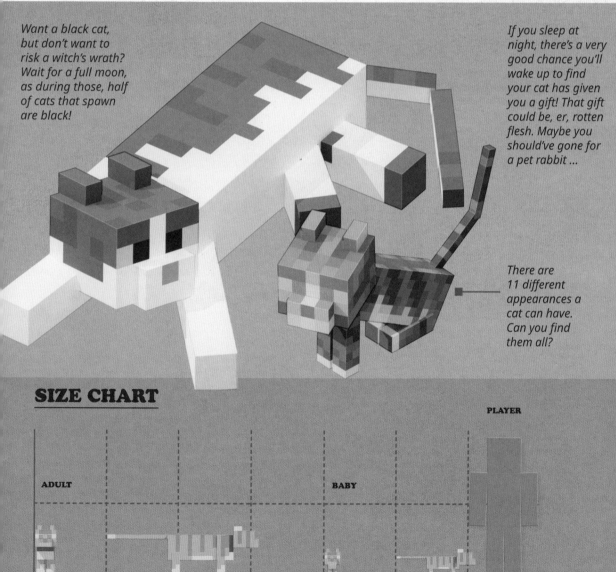

Want a black cat, but don't want to risk a witch's wrath? Wait for a full moon, as during those, half of cats that spawn are black!

If you sleep at night, there's a very good chance you'll wake up to find your cat has given you a gift! That gift could be, er, rotten flesh. Maybe you should've gone for a pet rabbit ...

There are 11 different appearances a cat can have. Can you find them all?

SIZE CHART

PLAYER

ADULT

BABY

IRON GOLEM

Looking for a bodyguard? Look no further – and not just because it's hard to look past the sheer intimidating bulk of the iron golem. These magnificent stacks of metal provide some much-needed muscle for villages all across the Overworld. But they also boast a softer side, occasionally offering ... a poppy? For us? You iron sweetheart!

"

Build your own bodyguard? Brilliant idea! This is one of the rare mobs that can actually be crafted by an adventurer. You simply need four iron blocks and a pumpkin to create an iron-based ally, and who WOULDN'T want that? I certainly feel more secure touring the villages of the Overworld, knowing I'm being protected by such a strong defender. Just be careful how you behave around villagers in the presence of an iron golem. I'm sure you're not one of those horrid people who would even dare consider harming a villager. But if you're foolish enough to do so, even if completely by accident, don't let the iron golem catch you ...

"

HABITAT

Iron golems spawn naturally in villages, where they act as the guardians of the peaceful villagers. Iron golems can also be found in pillager outposts under much sadder circumstances. They're trapped in dark oak cages. Luckily, if you break them out of the cages, they'll come to your aid and help you take down the pillagers. Nice!

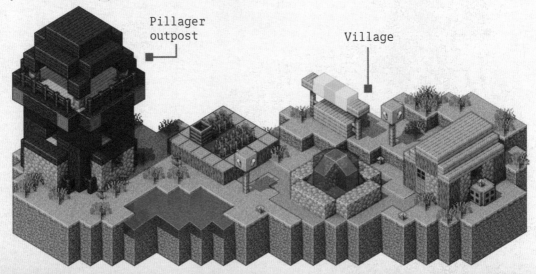

Pillager outpost

Village

■ *A golem offering a baby villager a poppy. Awww!*

MOB NOTES

OBSERVATIONS: Interestingly, iron golems won't leave their home village. They will protectively patrol their village borders, though.

DROPS: A defeated iron golem will drop up to 5 iron ingots. It may also drop a poppy or two, for you to remember them by!

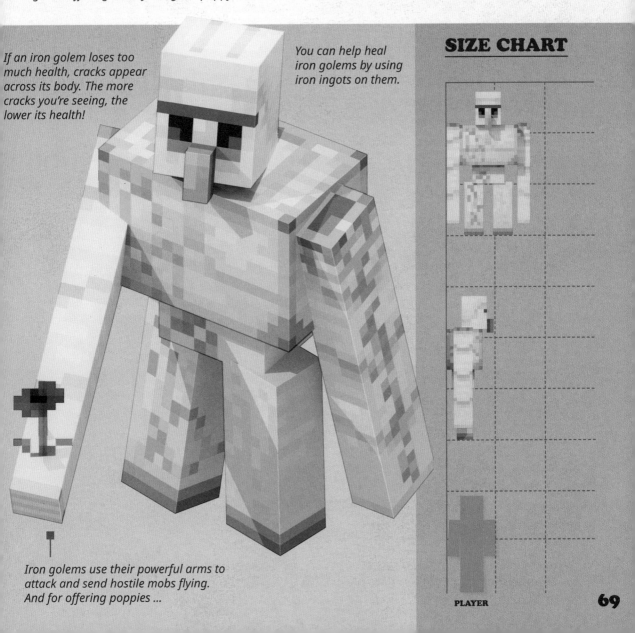

If an iron golem loses too much health, cracks appear across its body. The more cracks you're seeing, the lower its health!

You can help heal iron golems by using iron ingots on them.

SIZE CHART

Iron golems use their powerful arms to attack and send hostile mobs flying. And for offering poppies ...

WANDERING TRADER

This mysterious merchant in blue robes and with two llamas in tow will appear out of nowhere in the Overworld. But don't be alarmed! The wandering trader means you no harm – well, except maybe a little to your collection of emeralds. They spend their lives traversing the Overworld's biomes, trading their useful wares to adventurers. Flag one down and see what they've got on offer. Who knows? You might find something you've been searching for!

> *As a village researcher, I don't really like leaving the villages, especially because I'm also researching the scientific benefits of staying in bed all day. However, during my occasional travels from one village to the next, this magnificent merchant has gotten me out of many a pickle! They often offer items such as fish, dyes, plants and, er, sand blocks (thanks?). They're a great way of obtaining items without having to go on a dangerous journey to different distant biomes. Great news for my bed research! But not such great news for my rapidly dwindling emerald collection ...*

HABITAT

Wandering traders spawn in all Overworld biomes, so don't worry about searching for a specific biome to find one – just keep wandering the Overworld and you're certain to bump into one eventually, maybe even near your spawn point! But if you're desperate to trade, you can always seek out a village. The villagers there will also be more than happy to take your emeralds.

All Overworld biomes

■ *You'd feel safe wandering, too, if you had two llama bodyguards by your side.*

Wandering traders may resemble villagers but they can be found roaming across the entire Overworld, unlike villagers.

You will often hear wandering traders without seeing them. They occasionally drink a potion of Invisibility, usually at dusk or if they're attacked by hostile mobs. Smart!

You can't get the wandering trader to sell their llamas to you. That's blatant false advertising, trader!

SIZE CHART

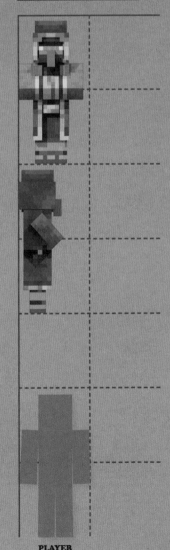

PLAYER

LLAMA
& TRADER LLAMA

Somehow managing to make wearing a carpet look cute, the llama and trader llama are very popular with explorers. After all, if you're looking for a colourful storage solution for those long trips from biome to biome, look no further! Just be sure to be on your best behaviour around llamas. Unless you want a free face-wash ...

> When a llama wears a carpet, they're considered adorable. if I wear a carpet, I get funny looks. Most unfair! Speaking of carpets, these charming beasts can wear any carpet you wish (the Enderman and creeper designs are my favourites). Just be careful when putting one on a llama, accidentally hurt one and you could spend the day avoiding their spit!

HABITAT

Your best bet of finding a regular llama is to seek out a savanna biome, as llamas spawn in the savanna, savanna plateau and windswept savanna (they're also a fan of the windswept hills biome). Trader llamas are unique and only spawn with wandering traders.

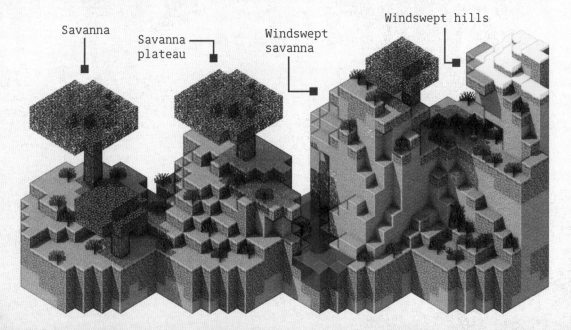

Savanna

Savanna plateau

Windswept savanna

Windswept hills

A llama spitting on a wolf. Ewww!

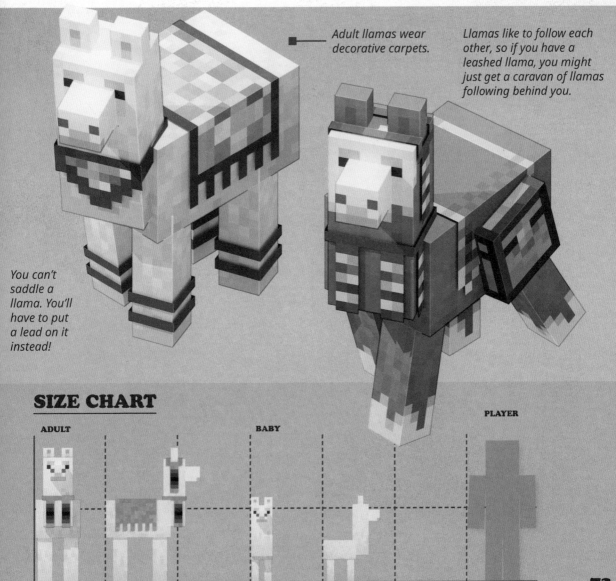

Adult llamas wear decorative carpets.

Llamas like to follow each other, so if you have a leashed llama, you might just get a caravan of llamas following behind you.

You can't saddle a llama. You'll have to put a lead on it instead!

SIZE CHART

ADULT

BABY

PLAYER

ALLAY

The little aqua-coloured cutie that lives to dance, the allay is an inspiration to us all. A lover of note blocks and playing fetch, this whimsical wisp will leave any explorer lucky enough to cross paths with it feeling far from blue! Oh, except for the slightly depressing fact that you can only find them in some of the most dangerous parts of the Overworld ...

> *What a fascinating mob this is! Give it an item and it'll fly off with it. HEY! But fret not, as the allay will soon return with more of whatever item you gave it! For example, I once gave an allay a piece of rotten flesh, and then moments later, I found myself with several more pieces of rotten flesh (and many regrets!). Even better, if you get a jukebox going, the allay will dance along with the music! It even puts MY mighty dance moves to shame. What's that? You agree that my dancing is terrible? Well don't be surprised if next time I have you over for dinner, I send the allay out for even more rotten flesh ...*

HABITAT

Exploring pillager outposts is always risky. But if you dare enter one, you may find allays locked within cages. Bring something that can smash open wood (which, er, you should definitely be wielding anyway if you're in pillager territory, friend) so you can set them free. Woodland mansions are very hard to discover, but you'll sometimes find allays in their cells. What crime did they commit? Being too cute? Relatable!

Pillager outpost

Woodland mansion

■ *Look at it dance! And it doesn't even have legs! Most impressive.*

MOB NOTES

OBSERVATIONS: These poor mobs are found imprisoned in cages. They deserve to fly free, so do the right thing!

DID YOU KNOW?: You wouldn't ever harm an allay, would you? Of course not! They don't drop any items when defeated – and are much more useful kept around!

The allay can seek out nearby items. Perfect for lazy adventurers! Ahem, not that we're implying YOU'RE lazy, of course.

Allays' bright colour can be seen clearly in the dark, even though they're not a source of light themselves. Huh!

If you have an amethyst shard, you can duplicate the allay! Hand it your shard while it's dancing and it'll play an amethyst sound and then you'll get another allay!

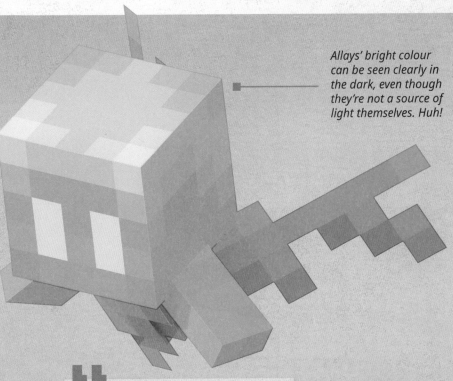

SIZE CHART

Despite being rare, allays are easy to spot. Their unique colour stands out well amongst many biomes.

PLAYER

PILLAGER

Pillagers wish you nothing but ill. These dark counterparts to the villagers are a hostile bunch indeed, armed with a dark grey complexion (no harm in that) and a crossbow (uh oh – lots of harm in that). It's up to you, noble explorer, to defend the villagers from the pillagers' attacks and ... hey, where are you going? Come back at once and protect me!

> *I was desperate to find somewhere for a nap when I suddenly heard a horn blowing, followed by a bell ringing. Oh boy – lunchtime! So imagine my disappointment when I wandered outside and had to settle for screaming in terror instead. It was a raid! Pillager after pillager flooded the village, firing their crossbows at yours truly! This was grim news, as I'm pretty sure I'm allergic to having crossbow bolts fired into me. So I picked up a sword and fought back. Afterwards, the villagers named me a hero of the village! Can you imagine that? Me? A hero!*

HABITAT

Pillagers mainly spawn in pillager outposts. These can be in any biome a village spawns in (plains, sunflower plains, snowy plains, desert, taiga, snowy taiga, savanna and meadow). As if that wasn't bad enough, they also spawn in the grove, snowy slopes, jagged peaks, stony peaks, frozen peaks and cherry groves. So it won't be long before you're face-to-face with them.

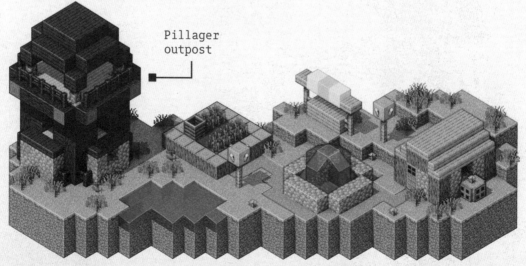

Pillager outpost

■ Pillager captains carry their own special banner, which can be seen on top of their heads.

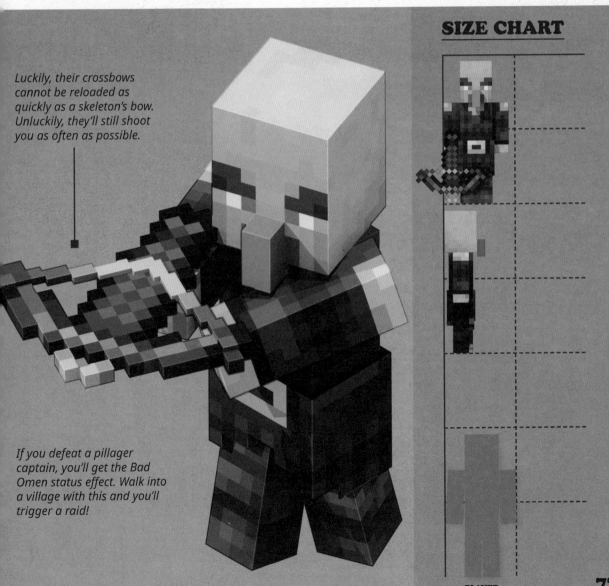

Luckily, their crossbows cannot be reloaded as quickly as a skeleton's bow. Unluckily, they'll still shoot you as often as possible.

If you defeat a pillager captain, you'll get the Bad Omen status effect. Walk into a village with this and you'll trigger a raid!

SIZE CHART

PLAYER

RAVAGER

he illager beast. The grumpiest cow. The stampeding jerk. These are just some of the names, spoken in petrified whispers, that have been given to the ravager (not that anyone has ever been foolish enough to say them to its face). Illagers love riding these intimidating creatures when charging into a village for a raid. The Overworld's most unpleasant mob? Again, we're not saying that to its massive face ...

> *Have you ever been caught up in a village raid? Truly terrifying! At least I feel like I have a chance against a pillager (well, sometimes). But the ravager is a foe beyond my capabilities. Ramming opponents with its humongous head is their nasty attack of choice. Those rams can knock back even a lovely researcher like myself by five blocks! Still, it's not just me they're attacking. They also ram iron golems, wandering traders and adult villagers. Nice of them to spare the children, I suppose, but I'd still better arm myself and be prepared to defend my villager hosts!*

HABITAT

Ravagers are only seen during raids. So to meet one, you'll need to get the Bad Omen status effect and then enter a village (remember, you can find one in the plains, sunflower plains, snowy plains, desert, taiga, snowy taiga, savanna and meadow). This will trigger a raid – survive until the third wave and you could meet a ravager.

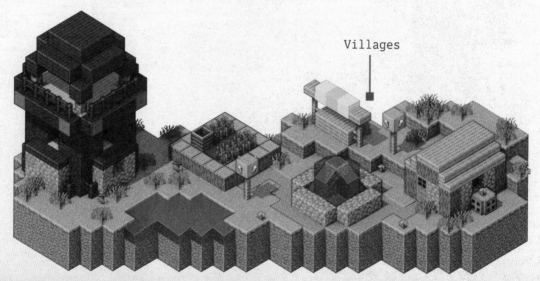

Villages

MOB NOTES

OBSERVATIONS: Ravagers aren't afraid of much, and they certainly won't shy away from ramming anything that's in their path. Even if it's you!

DROPS: These hostile beasts aren't easily defeated. If you manage to topple one, it will drop a saddle.

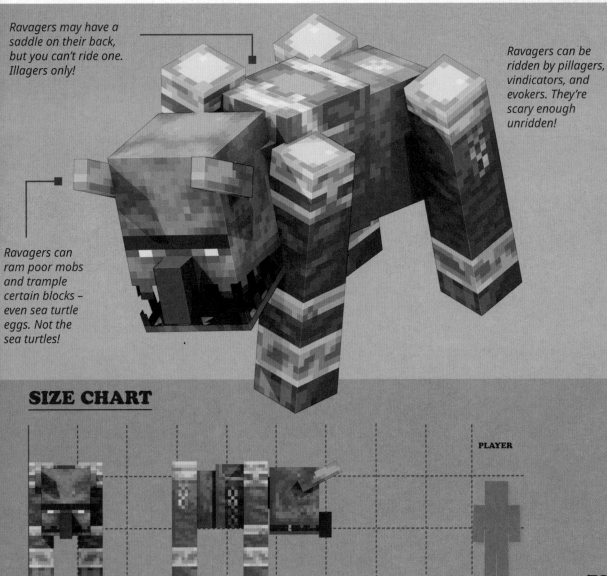

Ravagers may have a saddle on their back, but you can't ride one. Illagers only!

Ravagers can be ridden by pillagers, vindicators, and evokers. They're scary enough unridden!

Ravagers can ram poor mobs and trample certain blocks – even sea turtle eggs. Not the sea turtles!

SIZE CHART

PLAYER

EVOKER & VEX

Just like villagers, the evoker almost always has their arms crossed. Unlike villagers, this is because they have many nasty surprises hidden up their sleeves. This spellcaster can make fangs emerge from the ground, keen to chow down on you. It can also summon the vex, a sword-carrying, flying mob that might look like an allay, but is far, far more sinister.

> *Before I started exploring the villages of the Overworld, I had never witnessed magic with my own eyes! Unfortunately, the evoker's spells don't really care whether you're a newcomer to magic – you better believe that it'll hurt you anyway. Ouch! The vex is somehow even more horrid and it just had to be me to test their magic out, didn't it? I'm a nice person, aren't I? Wouldn't you rather read about a lovely evening I spent discussing great literature with myself, instead of reading about my miserable evenings spent getting attacked by a vex while an evoker giggled about my misfortune? No? Suit yourself ...*

HABITAT

Evokers spawn in woodland mansions and during wave five of a village raid. Woodland mansions are rare, but can be found in dark forest biomes. These mansions are not for the faint of heart, and they are the only other place where you'll find evokers and vindicators. Gulp!

Dark Forest

■ *The evoker's fang attack is better seen in photos than experienced for yourself.*

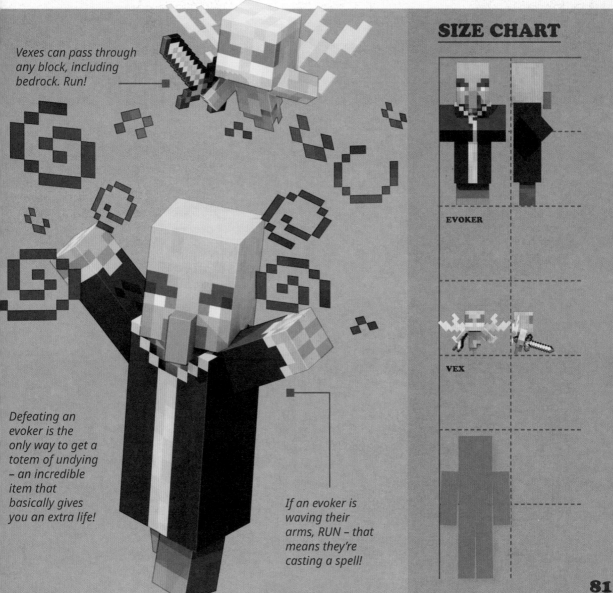

Vexes can pass through any block, including bedrock. Run!

Defeating an evoker is the only way to get a totem of undying – an incredible item that basically gives you an extra life!

If an evoker is waving their arms, RUN – that means they're casting a spell!

SIZE CHART

EVOKER

VEX

VINDICATOR

omeone with an axe running rapidly towards you is rarely good news, and sadly, a vindicator won't be approaching to help you chop down trees. No, this hostile mob is actually the strongest of the illagers. This lumberjack-gone-wrong is even capable of breaking down wooden doors, so cowering inside some poor villager's house is sadly not an option. Draw your sword, adventurer, and fight back!

What was that about how cowering inside a villager home is NOT an option? Vindicators often spawn during the later (significantly tougher!) waves of a raid. Sometimes they even spawn riding a ravager. Whereas I NEVER spawn riding a ravager. Not even once. Wait a minute ... I'm terrified of ravagers, I don't want to ride one! Anyway, I'd recommend using crossbows, bow and arrows or even some splash potions to fight vindicators – basically, anything you can use that keeps you nice and far away from the sharp end of their axe!

HABITAT

Vindicators spawn during village raids and can also be found in woodland mansions (rare structures that can be found in the dark forest biome). Proceed with extreme caution when exploring these structures – it's dark inside and vindicators' speed will take you by surprise.

Dark forest

■ *Quick. Stop them before they get to that poor villager!*

MOB NOTES

DROPS: Defeated vindicators drop emeralds and an Ominous banner, if they were a raid captain. They could also drop iron weapons, iron armour and an enchanted book.

DID YOU KNOW?: Vindicators are fearless. They'll take on mobs bigger than themselves, such as mighty iron golems.

Unlike other illager mobs, the vindicator's power is in their melee attacks.

If a pillager accidentally hits a vindicator with one of its arrows, the vindicator will attack it. Why not see if you can trick these mobs into fighting each other instead of you?

Vindicators can't walk at normal speeds, they can only sprint. This would be great news if they were sprinting away from you, rather than towards you ...

SIZE CHART

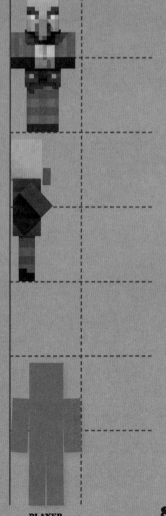

PLAYER

83

ZOMBIE VILLAGER

ombies are tragic enough, but seeing a poor villager that is now destined to shuffle across the Overworld as a zombie villager? That's enough to have us weeping for weeks. Similar in behaviour to the regular zombie, the crucial difference with zombie villagers is that they CAN be cured of their undead nightmare. So dry those tears, and restore them to life!

> *Just the other day, I was looking forward to a nice relaxing evening with the villagers, when a siege of zombies attacked the village. Luckily, we took care of them, but I was a bit worried that my neighbour had fallen ill. Were they always such a queasy shade of green? Why were they groaning whenever I told one of my hilarious jokes? After about six ticks of this I realised they were now a zombie villager! Luckily, I always carry several golden apples in my inventory. With a potion of Weakness and one of these, a zombie villager will soon become a regular villager. Hooray! Hopefully they'll stop moaning so much now!*

HABITAT

Except for the mushroom fields and deep dark, zombies can be found in every Overworld biome. When a group spawns, there's a small chance of it being a group of zombie villagers. You can also encounter groups of these in an abandoned village, which can be found in any biomes that spawn villages. Alternatively, if a zombie defeats a villager, there's a chance of that villager turning into a zombie villager. Yikes!

Almost all
Overworld biomes

OBSERVATIONS: They might be frightening, but zombie villager's can be cured with golden apples and potions of Weakness ... or defeated with a sword or bow!

DROPS: They will often drop rotten flesh, but there's also a small chance they'll drop an iron ingot, a carrot or a potato.

■ *Oh sure, this looks adorable now – but not when it catches up to you ... and it will.*

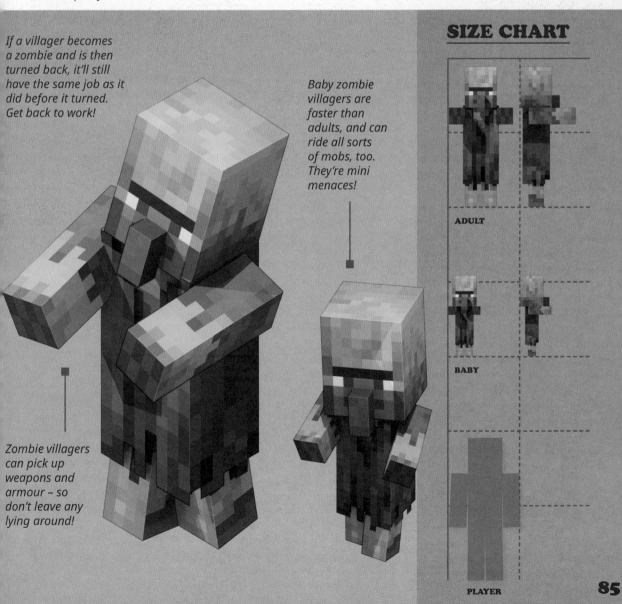

If a villager becomes a zombie and is then turned back, it'll still have the same job as it did before it turned. Get back to work!

Baby zombie villagers are faster than adults, and can ride all sorts of mobs, too. They're mini menaces!

SIZE CHART

ADULT

BABY

PLAYER

Zombie villagers can pick up weapons and armour – so don't leave any lying around!

WITCH

Minecraft's most stylish hat has somehow found itself upon the head of one of the Overworld's meanest mobs. The witch is a master of potions. Sadly, they've used that mastery to spread havoc, lobbing their little glass bottles of misery at explorers. Either keep your distance, or swot up on your potion-brewing abilities to turn the tables!

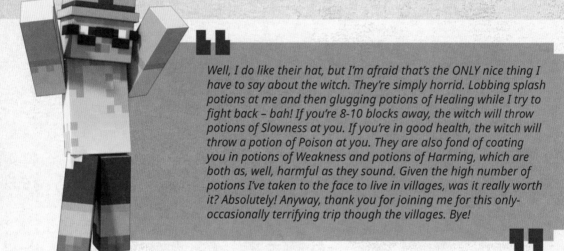

> Well, I do like their hat, but I'm afraid that's the ONLY nice thing I have to say about the witch. They're simply horrid. Lobbing splash potions at me and then glugging potions of Healing while I try to fight back – bah! If you're 8-10 blocks away, the witch will throw potions of Slowness at you. If you're in good health, the witch will throw a potion of Poison at you. They are also fond of coating you in potions of Weakness and potions of Harming, which are both as, well, harmful as they sound. Given the high number of potions I've taken to the face to live in villages, was it really worth it? Absolutely! Anyway, thank you for joining me for this only-occasionally terrifying trip though the villages. Bye!

HABITAT

Witches can spawn at night in all Overworld biomes (except mushroom fields and the deep dark) and anywhere with low light, such as caves. They occur during village raids, and villagers who are struck by lightning will transform into witches. Swamp biomes are also worth seeking out (or avoiding), as witches will spawn in swamp huts.

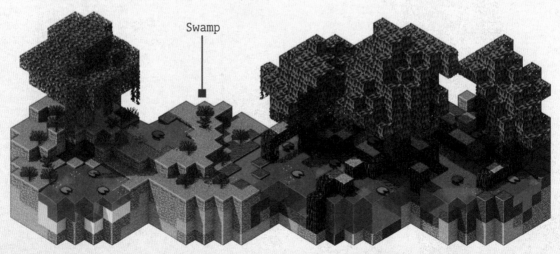

Swamp

It's never a potion of 'wellbeing' or 'free emeralds' being thrown at us, is it?

MOB NOTES

OBSERVATIONS: Among the places you can expect to find a witch is wave four of a village raid ... if you've made it that far!

DID YOU KNOW?: Witches drop several items. Sticks, glass bottles, redstone dust, glowstone dust, spider eyes, gunpowder, sugar and even a potion they were holding!

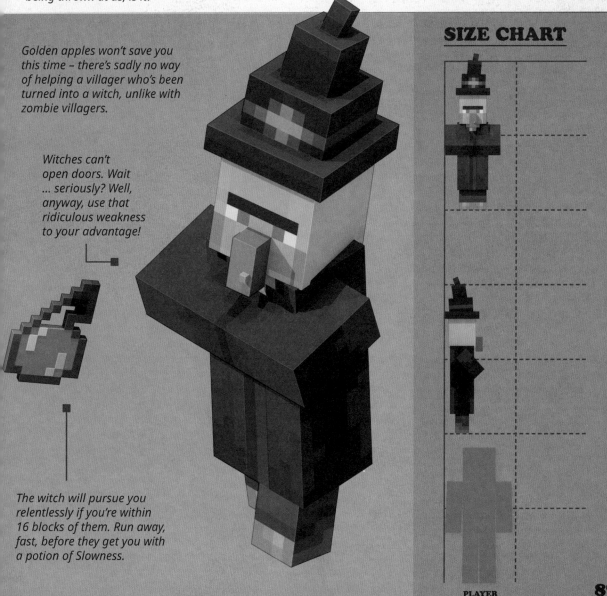

Golden apples won't save you this time – there's sadly no way of helping a villager who's been turned into a witch, unlike with zombie villagers.

Witches can't open doors. Wait ... seriously? Well, anyway, use that ridiculous weakness to your advantage!

The witch will pursue you relentlessly if you're within 16 blocks of them. Run away, fast, before they get you with a potion of Slowness.

SIZE CHART

EXTREME TRAVELLERS

Hi there, ground-dwellers! Oh, sorry – didn't mean to be rude. That's what we mountain folk call you lot down there! See, I was raised in a remote village in the hills. Did you know I learned to climb before I learned to talk? It didn't make me very popular at parties ... but there aren't many parties on mountaintops anyway. Look, I'm not just obsessed with higher ground – I also love to see what mysterious mobs are lurking beneath the surface!

So strap on your climbing boots, pack your pickaxe and join me, Heidi Peaks, on an adventure!

BAT

Cave-dwelling rats with wings? Hardly! For the bat wishes you no harm at all. These misunderstood mobs are completely passive. They enjoy hanging from blocks, squeaking and sometimes flapping around aimlessly. They may not be winning a cuteness competitions anytime soon, and they might make you jump, but they're no threat to explorers. Caves really wouldn't be the same without them!

■

> *I don't just hang out on top of mountains – I'm a big fan of caving inside and underneath them, too! Especially because it means I have to deal with bats ... which is great! I LOVE bats! They're small, they're squeaky and ... they occasionally, accidentally fly into lava! I just think digging deep into a dark cave would lose some of its spooky magic without these little guys flapping around. Some RUDE people think I'm weird for liking bats ... and because I wrote a 6,000-page novel called 'BATS ARE DA BEST'. Okay, they might have a point about me being weird.*

HABITAT

You'll have to break out your pickaxe and shovel and get exploring if you want to meet some bats. They need dark and the underground to spawn, so if both of those simple criteria are met, it won't be long before you see some darting about.

Underground

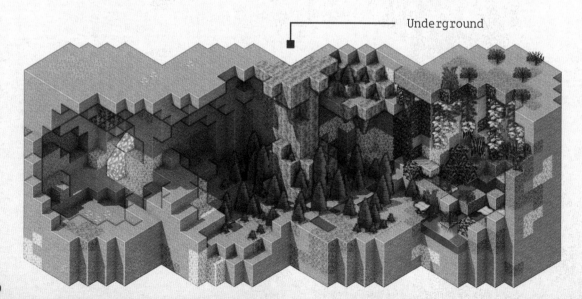

■ *A bat hanging from a block. Don't break that block!*

MOB NOTES

OBSERVATIONS: It's unknown if bats are afraid of lava – but they should be. They have been seen flying tragically into it.
DID YOU KNOW?: These tiny mobs are often found in groups of two. If you see one flying around a cave, there's a good chance another will be hanging close by.

Even if you approach a bat after drinking a potion of Invisibility, it will still fly away.

For unknown reasons, bats tend to fly to the east. You could use this to navigate if you're lost!

A bat's defeated sound is a particularly horrible screech. Gah!

SIZE CHART

Despite having smaller bodies than many mobs, bats appear larger thanks to their impressive wingspan.

PLAYER

FOX

This orange-and-white wonder is beloved by all. Well, except maybe if you're a chicken. Or a chicken farmer. Or just a general fan of chickens living long and healthy lives. Oh, or a rabbit or a turtle. Otherwise, you're likely a fan of the fox! This furry friend has leapt into many an explorer's heart, but you will need to be eagle-eyed to see one, as they are incredibly elusive creatures.

I spend a lot of time strolling through the snowy taiga. We get white foxes, because those are the ones that spawn in snowy biomes. I'm not complaining! These cuties are a delight to come across. Sometimes I see them pounce and land headfirst in a snow layer, where they get stuck! They'll shake around for a little while until they get free (and I ALWAYS stick around to make sure they get free). These white foxes have more of a taste for fish than their reddish counterparts – and are also more camouflaged in their biomes. The red fox may be much easier to spot, but they are still rare.

HABITAT

White foxes spawn in the snowy taiga. Orange-and-white foxes spawn in the old growth taigas, taiga and grove biomes. So, er, maybe don't start your chicken farm in any of those biomes. Or your baby turtle sanctuary. If you're lucky, you might witness them stalking unsuspecting prey through tall spruce trees.

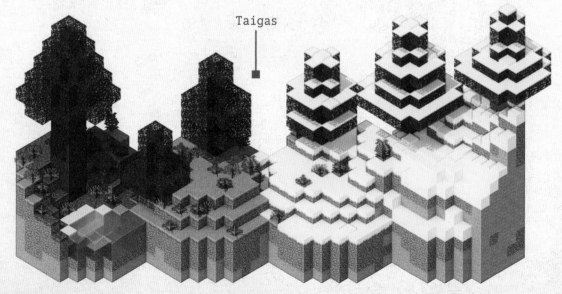

Taigas

■ *The fox uses a unique jumping attack method.*

Thanks to its strong jaw, a fox can pick up items in its mouth, grabbing anything it finds, but will drop it if food becomes available.

Strong legs provide a burst of speed and a mighty jump, perfect for its unique style of attack.

When foxes sleep, their heads move up and down but they'll somehow sense if you get too close.

SIZE CHART

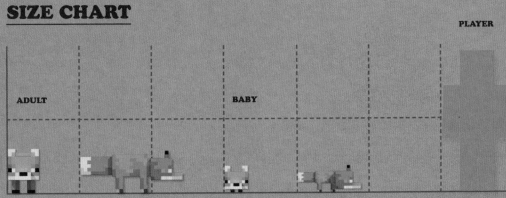

PLAYER

ADULT

BABY

POLAR BEAR

Think twice before messing with the offspring of the polar bear (and those thoughts should be 'run' and 'away', if you value your life). This protective parent may look warm and fuzzy, but it's not afraid to attack anyone foolish enough to mess with its kids. Not that anyone horrible enough to attack a baby polar bear would be reading a book as fun as this one ... right?

> *I'd sooner eat my hood than attack a baby polar bear. So I thought I'd be safe to explore their biomes without one taking a swipe at me. Wrong. Very wrong! Getting too close to an adult polar bear (I only wanted a selfie!) is all it takes for it to become hostile. If you see one rear up onto its back legs, it's about to come down on you with paws full of claws! I tried swimming away, but that's no good, as their swim speed is just as strong as yours! Luckily, I got away so I could start writing this. Wait ... how DID I get away? Uh-oh, I forgot to run away. It's right there!!!*

HABITAT

Polar bears are fond of biomes full of snow and ice. You'll find them in the snowy plains, ice spikes, frozen ocean, deep frozen ocean, frozen rivers, frozen peaks, jagged peaks and snowy slopes. Try not to slip on all that ice if you suddenly find yourself having to flee them!

```
Almost all snow
and ice biomes
```

■ *If you see a polar bear in the wild doing this, perhaps start making funeral preparations.*

MOB NOTES

OBSERVATIONS: Polar bear cubs may start their life as passive mobs, but they become neutral as adults – so they won't react well if you cause them any harm!

DID YOU KNOW?: You may not want to defeat a polar bear, but, if you do, they can drop raw salmon or raw cod. Tasty!

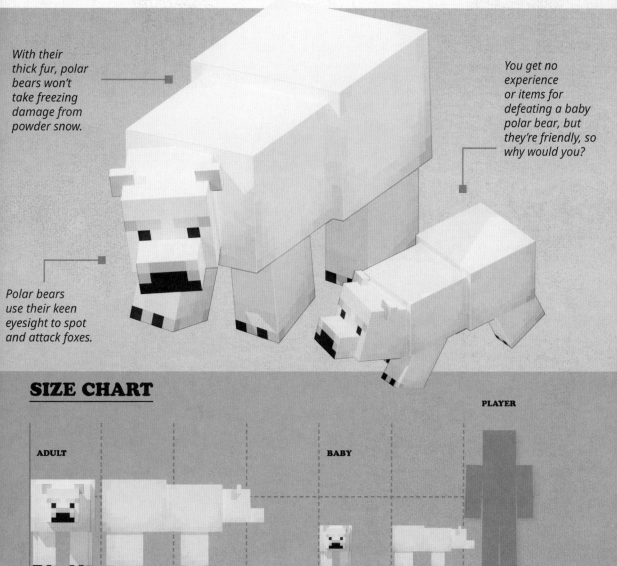

With their thick fur, polar bears won't take freezing damage from powder snow.

You get no experience or items for defeating a baby polar bear, but they're friendly, so why would you?

Polar bears use their keen eyesight to spot and attack foxes.

SIZE CHART

PLAYER

ADULT

BABY

SNOW GOLEM

Looks can be deceiving, and few mobs showcase that better than the pumpkin-headed horror that is the snow golem. Ah, but it's not a horror at all! Despite a face that even a creeper might find gloomy, this passive pal is a mob you can build yourself that will happily protect you. It really is a superior snowman that won't leave you feeling frosty!

All you need is two snow blocks and then either a pumpkin, carved pumpkin or jack o'lantern for the head. Then voilà! Your snowman will come alive! Better still, the snow golem will become your bodyguard. They'll throw snowballs at hostile mobs! Er, even when you don't want them to. Their attacks are pretty weak – a snowball just doesn't have the same impact as an arrow or a sword swing – so you'll probably have to step in and help your frosty friend out in the fight. Awww, but snowball fights are so much more fun!

HABITAT

Their habitat is wherever you want it to be, but you'll find the snow blocks you'll need in ice spikes, grove, snowy slopes, frozen peaks and jagged peaks biomes. You can find pumpkins in grassy biomes, so it shouldn't be too difficult to find one.

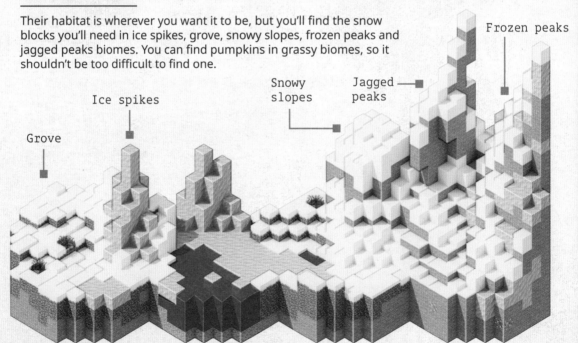

Frozen peaks

Snowy slopes

Jagged peaks

Ice spikes

Grove

■ *Look at that cute smile! At least ... we think it's a smile?*

MOB NOTES

OBSERVATIONS: Snow golems wander aimlessly, but they will avoid obstacles and environmental damage.

DROPS: When a snow golem is defeated, it can drop up to 15 snowballs. You might enjoy throwing them, but they don't cause much damage!

Shear the pumpkin on a snow golem and you'll reveal its lovely smiling face!

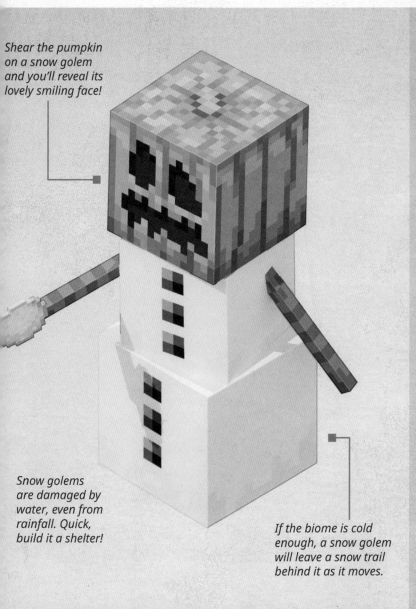

Snow golems are damaged by water, even from rainfall. Quick, build it a shelter!

If the biome is cold enough, a snow golem will leave a snow trail behind it as it moves.

SIZE CHART

PLAYER

SILVERFISH

Why is this stone block taking a suspiciously long time to break with a pickaxe? It may be because you're mining an infested block – and breaking it open has released the silverfish sneakily hiding inside. These miniature hostile mobs are a stone mason's worst nightmare. Precious-metal fans shouldn't be fooled by the 'silver' in the name, nor should fishermen get intrigued by the 'fish' in it either, for these slithery mobs wish you nothing but pain!

> *Ewwww! Look, I try to admire all of the Overworld's various creepies and crawlies, but the silverfish is a really tough mob to love! There I am, innocently chipping away at a stone block under a mountain, not a care in the world – when suddenly a silverfish pops out and attacks me! Actually, to be fair, I DID just destroy its home ... but still! Silverfish will slither across the floor, attempting to bite you. And if you fight back, then all its fellow silverfish will attack you, too! Look, I know I'm going a little overboard with the exclamation marks here. But it's the silverfish, you guys! They really!!! Freak!!! Me!!! Out!!!*

HABITAT

Silverfish spawn when infested blocks are broken. These blocks can be found in windswept gravelly hills, windswept hills, and windswept forest, and are also possible in meadows, groves, snowy slopes, jagged peaks, frozen peaks and stony peaks. You can also find them in structures, such as woodland mansions, strongholds and igloo basements.

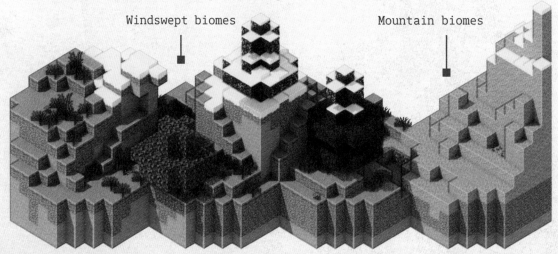

Windswept biomes ↓   Mountain biomes ↓

■ *I told you to mine more cautiously, friend!*

MOB NOTES

OBSERVATIONS: Move with caution in areas known to be home to silverfish. They can see you through walls, so are you ever safe?

DID YOU KNOW?: Silverfish drop nothing when they are defeated. Cause them damage and they'll call for backup from other silverfish in the area. Gah!

Idle silverfish can infest other blocks, transforming them into infested blocks. So make sure you finish them off properly!

If you damage a silverfish but don't defeat it, all nearby silverfish will burst out of their infected blocks. Eeek!

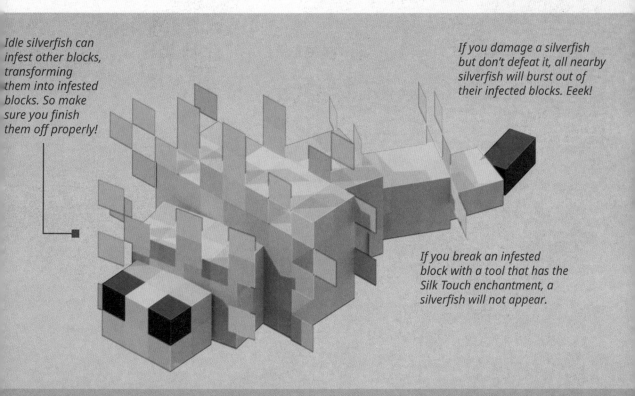

If you break an infested block with a tool that has the Silk Touch enchantment, a silverfish will not appear.

SIZE CHART

PLAYER

SLIME

A creepy cube that shouldn't be underestimated, the slime is one of the Overworld's oddest hostile mobs. These lime squares bounce around, jumping on their enemies to attack them. Sadly, their enemies include you, but fear not – they're not too tough to defeat in battle. Just one thing ... defeat a slime and it will split into more smaller slimes!

Anyone else getting a craving for trampolining from looking at this mob? No? Just me? Suit yourselves. Slimes can be a right nuisance when you're exploring. Did you know they can swim through water, climb ladders and even climb scaffolding? They're so persistent! I'm not THAT famous ... Usually the best course of action is to draw my sword and fight back. However, slimes split in two when defeated – and sometimes they even split into FOUR. Suddenly you're in four times as much trouble! Sure, these new slimes are half the size of the original slime, but that just makes them harder to hit. Oh, why is it never cats who want to follow me, huh? It's always evil green cubes!

HABITAT

Slimes spawn most often in the swamp biome. Interestingly enough, they spawn far more often on a full moon. Do they possess werewolf DNA? Are they big fans of the lunar calendar? Or do they just like a full moon? It's a mystery we may never solve. With the exception of mushroom fields and the deep dark, slimes can spawn in all Overworld biomes.

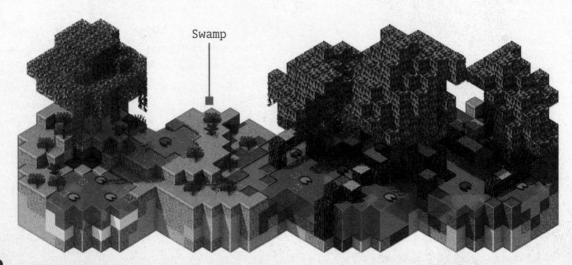

Swamp

■ *Oh no! I've ended up with several slimy foes!*

MOB NOTES

OBSERVATIONS: They might be a real nuisance, but slimes aren't that tough. If they were, frogs wouldn't be able to eat them with such ease.

DID YOU KNOW?: When a slime is finally defeated, it will drop slimeballs – used to craft sticky pistons and magma cream.

Slimes aren't just hostile to you. They also attack iron golems. Perhaps they're jealous of a mob that's built of something more sturdy?

Put a name tag on a slime and if you vanquish it, the smaller slimes it produces will have the same name!

The smallest slimes will still attack you, but won't do any attack damage. Awww! Nice try, little guys!

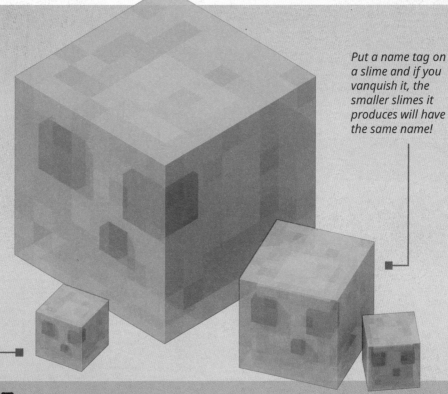

SIZE CHART

BIG		MEDIUM	SMALL			PLAYER	

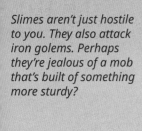

HUSK

ombies are supposed to burn in sunlight, but one type of zombie didn't get the memo. The husk has no fear of catching some rays while it's trying to catch you, which makes it one of the more frightening threats you can encounter while exploring the desert. Now daylight won't come to your rescue, you'll have to think of a new strategy to overcome this undeterred undead! Groan, nothing's ever easy.

My friends kept saying I should broaden my horizons and try exploring a biome I don't go to much. So I went on holiday to the desert! Remind me when I get home to get new friends. If I survive, that is, because this desolate desert is full of hostile husks! These zombie variants don't take damage from sunlight, whereas my skin, from a lifetime of living in snowy mountains, doesn't like this desert sun one bit! Did you know that when a husk successfully hits you, you get more hungry? And did you also know that there are no decent restaurants in the Overworld's deserts? Worst holiday ever!

HABITAT

As poor Heidi has discovered, husks are very much creatures of the desert biome. 70% of zombies that spawn in the desert biome will be husks. If you're planning on wandering the desert when the sun goes down, bring plenty of weapons and snacks!

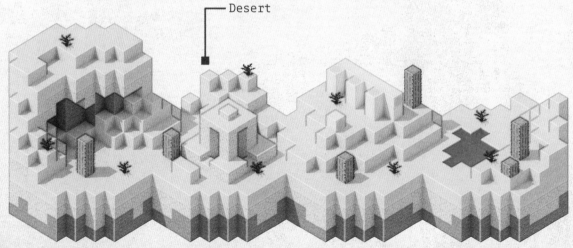

Desert

■ *A husk happily basking in the sun's rays.*

MOB NOTES

OBSERVATIONS: Like all zombie variants, husks will pursue you from much further away than most other hostile mobs – so always keep an eye out!

DROPS: Husks drop rotten flesh upon defeat. You could eat this, but you risk inflicting Hunger.

Although it resembles the zombie, a husk's colour suits its desert surroundings.

A husk that's underwater for thirty seconds transforms into a normal zombie. You'll have to wait another thirty seconds for it to become a drowned (er, but wouldn't you rather use that time to run away?).

SIZE CHART

ADULT

BABY

PLAYER

CAVE SPIDER

A smaller spider variant, perfect for squeezing through cramped caverns, the cave spider has been the poisonous end of many an adventurer. Don't let the fact they're smaller than the average spider fool you, for they're significantly more deadly. Their attacks poison you, which, according to several doctors we contacted for this book, is 'bad for you'. Fascinating!

> "Hot take time: I LOVE cave spiders! Now I know that's not a very popular opinion. In fact, it's probably why people have stopped coming to my place for dinner. Well, that, and the fact I live on the peak of a mountain. And I won't shut up about how cool spiders are. Anyway, I get that not everyone is a fan of being poisoned, or having to walk through sticky cobwebs, or the TERRIFYING sounds that cave spiders make. But caves wouldn't be the same without them! Maybe it's just me, but I like a bit of menace in my Overworld. It makes survival all the more satisfying!"

HABITAT

Cave spiders spawn from monster spawners found in mineshafts. These mineshafts are almost always found underground in caves (except for in the badlands, where a unique dark oak wood variant can generate overground), and it could well take you a long time to locate one.

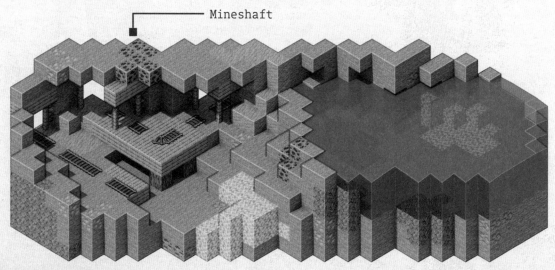

Mineshaft

■ *Our photographer quit seconds after taking this photo. We can't blame them.*

MOB NOTES

OBSERVATIONS: Monster spawners can be found in in many places, but those in mineshafts will spawn these terrifying cave-dwellers!

DROPS: Cave spiders may drop string when they're defeated. There is also a good chance that they'll drop a spider eye!

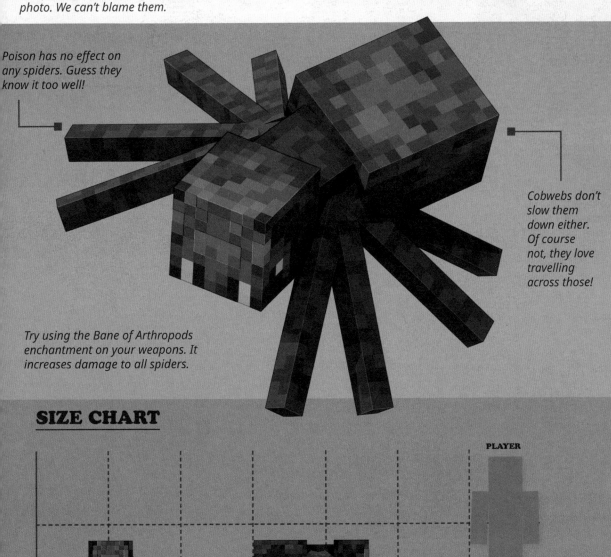

Poison has no effect on any spiders. Guess they know it too well!

Cobwebs don't slow them down either. Of course not, they love travelling across those!

Try using the Bane of Arthropods enchantment on your weapons. It increases damage to all spiders.

SIZE CHART

PLAYER

STRAY

The Overworld's colder biomes get a mob that is wearing torn rags that show off their empty ribcage. The stray is a scary skeleton that's determined to slow you down – avoid their magical arrows if you can, or your speedy walk through the snow might turn into a plodding death march ...

"

If this was 'The Big Book of Minecraft Fashion Fails' then the stray would likely feature on the cover. Skeletons of the snowy biomes have no need to wrap up warm, I suppose, but is that really an excuse for dressing in such drab grey rags? Ouch! Hey, they just shot me with an arrow for being so shallow! Suddenly ... I ... feel ... slow ... er? Uh oh! That's because the arrows a stray fires inflict Slowness upon you for 30 seconds after you're hit. 30 seconds might not sound like a long time, but with hostile mobs closing in, it can be the time between life and death! Um, actually strays, now I look a little closer, I love your outfits! So bravely bland! Ow, ow, ow! Yeah, I didn't think that would work ...

"

HABITAT

Strays naturally spawn in the snowy plains biome, but it's the icier places of the Overworld where you'll frequently encounter these most chilling of foes. They spawn in frozen oceans, deep frozen oceans, frozen rivers and ice spikes. Some of those biomes were plenty treacherous already, so make sure you're on your guard!

```
Snow and
ice biomes
```

MOB NOTES

OBSERVATIONS: If you're in an icy biome, you're much more likely to encounter a stray instead of the usual skeleton variant.

DID YOU KNOW?: They sometimes drop their enchanted arrows of Slowness when defeated, as well as bones, arrows and any equipment they might have picked up.

■ *Our new photographer sadly took an arrow to the face to get this photo. Um, welcome to the team!*

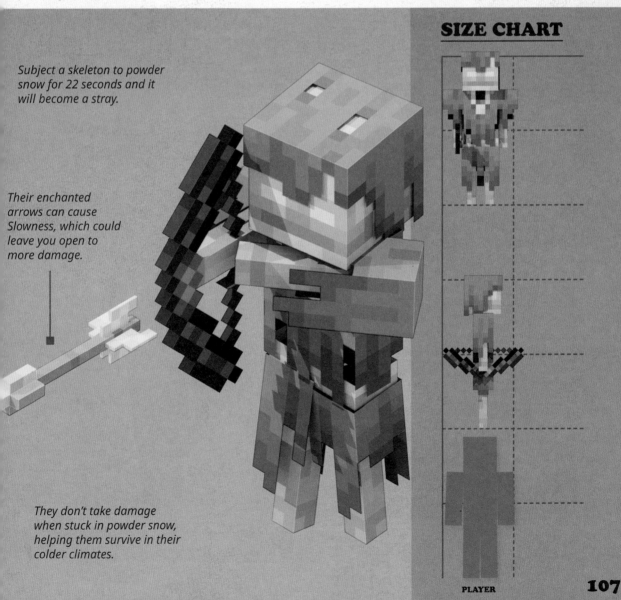

Subject a skeleton to powder snow for 22 seconds and it will become a stray.

Their enchanted arrows can cause Slowness, which could leave you open to more damage.

They don't take damage when stuck in powder snow, helping them survive in their colder climates.

SIZE CHART

WARDEN

A mob so dangerous that we can't ethically recommend you even read about it without putting on enchanted armour first. The warden deals the highest melee damage of all the mobs, and has the highest health. As if a physical smack from it isn't bad enough (it is), its sonic boom attacks can bypass blocks AND enchanted armour. Oh. Guess that armour was no help at all. Sorry, hopefully these pages will better prepare you!

> *You want me to say something? Out loud? About the warden, a sightless mob with great hearing that hates being disturbed?! OK, but this feels like a trap ... I like to think I'm pretty brave, but exploring the deep dark is absolutely terrifying with this monster lurking about! The trick to getting past the warden is to make as little noise as possible, which isn't easy when all you want to do is sprint. Although my habit of humming and singing as I explore is REALLY not helping me out down here. Oh! This is my last page of the book! Better say a big GOOODBYE!!! Uh oh. That probably wasn't a good idea either ...*

HABITAT

The warden is the biggest mob of the deep dark, a cave biome that's deep underground, and the good news is that you won't find one lurking in any other biome. Known for its poor lighting and even poorer survival prospects, the deep dark has sculk sensors, which will trigger sculk shriekers. Set those off, and the warden will happily introduce itself. Rather you than us ...

Deep dark

If it cannot reach you, its secondary attack is a primary problem for explorers!

MOB NOTES

OBSERVATIONS: The warden will only spawn once you trigger four sculk shriekers. You'll trigger them even when sneaking – so watch your step!

DROPS: Defeat a warden and it will drop one sculk catalyst. Your chance to take a piece of the deep dark home ...

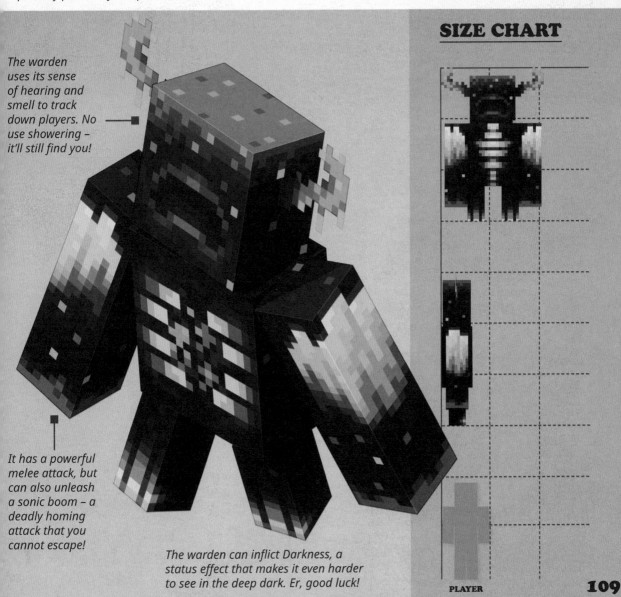

The warden uses its sense of hearing and smell to track down players. No use showering – it'll still find you!

It has a powerful melee attack, but can also unleash a sonic boom – a deadly homing attack that you cannot escape!

The warden can inflict Darkness, a status effect that makes it even harder to see in the deep dark. Er, good luck!

SIZE CHART

PLAYER

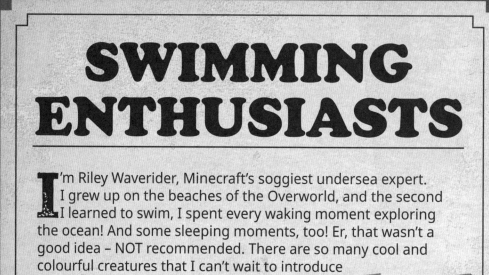

SWIMMING ENTHUSIASTS

I'm Riley Waverider, Minecraft's soggiest undersea expert. I grew up on the beaches of the Overworld, and the second I learned to swim, I spent every waking moment exploring the ocean! And some sleeping moments, too! Er, that wasn't a good idea – NOT recommended. There are so many cool and colourful creatures that I can't wait to introduce you to in this, easily the wettest, section of the book (hopefully not literally, try to keep your copy dry if you can). I'll warn you now that not all ocean life is friendly and I know from experience that there are monsters in those murky depths – that can swim fast and throw tridents even faster! But don't worry ... it's time to get your swimming costume on and dive in!

COD & SALMON

A couple of the Overworld's most plentiful fish also have the bad luck of being two of its tastiest. Cod and salmon are the meal of choice for cats, ocelots and any adventurer who forgot to pack their lunch before going for a dip. Any aspiring fisherman keen to tame themselves a feline friend should consider seeking out cod and salmon – cats and ocelots love fish!

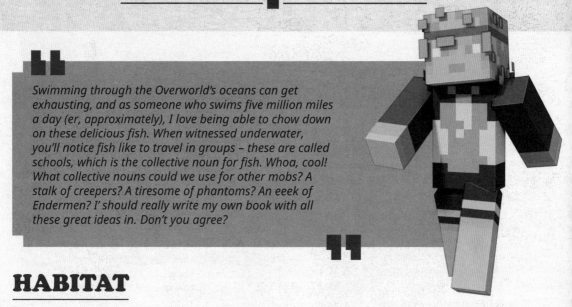

Swimming through the Overworld's oceans can get exhausting, and as someone who swims five million miles a day (er, approximately), I love being able to chow down on these delicious fish. When witnessed underwater, you'll notice fish like to travel in groups – these are called schools, which is the collective noun for fish. Whoa, cool! What collective nouns could we use for other mobs? A stalk of creepers? A tiresome of phantoms? An eeek of Endermen? I' should really write my own book with all these great ideas in. Don't you agree?

HABITAT

Both cod and salmon are common sights if you're swimming in an ocean biome. They spawn in lukewarm, cold, normal and frozen oceans, and the deep versions of all those biomes, too. Salmon also spawn in rivers, so if you're only looking for salmon (hey, what have you got against cod?) grab your fishing rod and spend a sunny afternoon by the river. Bliss!

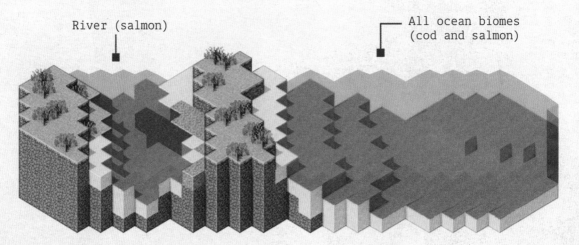

River (salmon)

All ocean biomes (cod and salmon)

MOB NOTES

OBSERVATIONS: You will see salmon swimming in schools of up to five, and cod in schools of up to seven, perfect for a comforting meal if you're lost at sea!

DROPS: Defeated cod could drop raw cod, bones and even bonemeal. Salmon will drop raw salmon or bones.

■ *Our photographer didn't want to get wet, so they took photos of fish in buckets instead.*

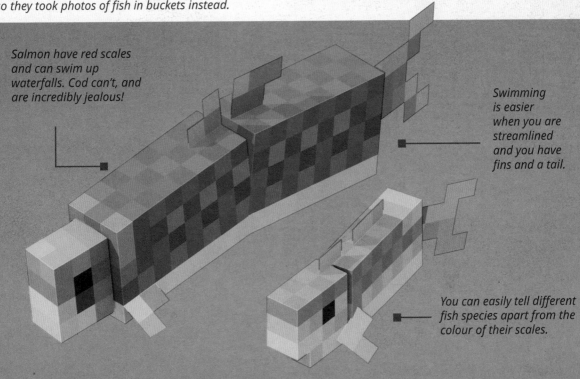

Salmon have red scales and can swim up waterfalls. Cod can't, and are incredibly jealous!

Swimming is easier when you are streamlined and you have fins and a tail.

You can easily tell different fish species apart from the colour of their scales.

SIZE CHART

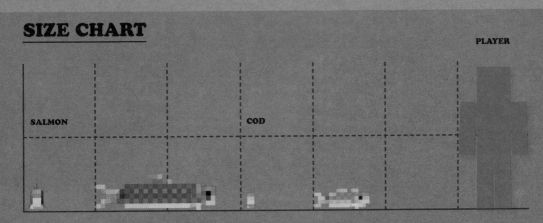

PLAYER

SALMON

COD

AXOLOTL

Winner of 'most frequently double-checked spelling while writing this book' award, the axolotl is also a strong candidate for the cutest water-dwelling mob. It adds a powerful punch of pastel-coloured prettiness to even the palest pools. Perfection! Unless, of course, it's secretly one of waters most dangerous predators, hiding behind a cute facade ... But that can't be true! Can it?

———————— ■ ————————

> *I was so excited to meet the adorable axolotl, but imagine my horrified gasps when I saw that the axolotl is passive towards adventurers, but hostile towards some other aquatic mobs! Please do imagine my gasps by the way, because it's never a good idea to literally gasp underwater. Unless you're an explorer, turtle, dolphin, frog or another axolotl, this cutie is cut-throat! It will even attack drowned. I won't ever attack drowned – I'm too terrified of tridents!*

HABITAT

If you've got aspirations of seeing axolotls, you'll need to find a lush cave. These generate most often under humid biomes, such as dark forests, jungles and wooded badlands. If you're in a very humid biome, such as old growth taiga or bamboo jungle, you've got a very high chance of finding a lush cave below! Azalea trees generate above lush caves, so keep an eye out for them and you'll soon discover a cute, little axolotl.

Lush cave ⎯⎤
                ▪

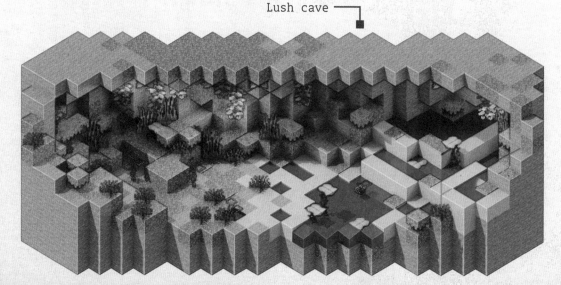

MOB NOTES

OBSERVATIONS: They might be passive, but these cuties can assist you if you're engaged in combat with many other aquatic mobs.

DID YOU KNOW?: When an axolotl receives damage underwater, there is a small chance that it will drop to the ground and play dead, so that its opponent leaves it alone.

■ *Whoa, axolotls are WAY braver than us! We couldn't even take this photo without trembling.*

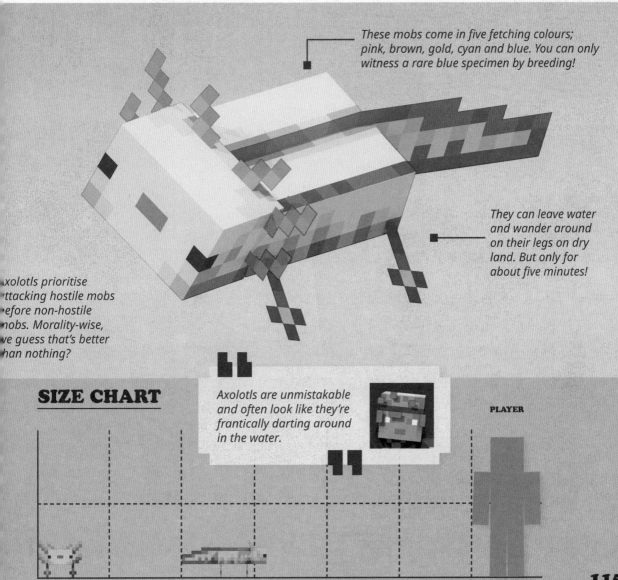

These mobs come in five fetching colours; pink, brown, gold, cyan and blue. You can only witness a rare blue specimen by breeding!

They can leave water and wander around on their legs on dry land. But only for about five minutes!

Axolotls prioritise attacking hostile mobs before non-hostile mobs. Morality-wise, we guess that's better than nothing?

SIZE CHART

Axolotls are unmistakable and often look like they're frantically darting around in the water.

PLAYER

SEA TURTLE

Quite possibly the Overworld's greatest reason to visit the beach. The sea turtle is something of a slowpoke on land, but a lean, green, speed machine in the sea. These harmless mobs have a surprisingly high number of enemies, with many hostile mobs attacking them, their baby variants and even their eggs. It's your solemn duty to defend the sea turtles and their offspring, explorer!

Just like the sea turtle, I'm pretty slow on land, but super speedy in the water (I just don't GET land, OK?). The thing I love most about them is that they never forget their home beach. No matter where they are in the entire Overworld, after breeding, they'll ALWAYS seek out the block they were born on, so they can lay their eggs there. Isn't that incredible? They literally remember where they were born! Whereas I can barely remember what I had for breakfast! When a baby sea turtle reaches adulthood, it drops a scute, which can be used to craft a turtle shell helmet that allows you to stay underwater for longer!

HABITAT

You'll find sea turtles and their eggs on beaches (but not snowy beaches or stony shores). They can also frequently be spotted underwater, but strolling across the Overworld's sunnier shores is still your best bet of finding one. Plus, if you seek them out on land, there's no way they'll outrun you! Well, unless you're REALLY slow ...

Beach

■ *Back off, zombie. We said back off!*

MOB NOTES

OBSERVATIONS: It appears that almost every hostile mob will attack baby turtles, turtles or their eggs. They need protection!

DROPS: Sea turtles may drop seagrass and, if they were defeated by lightning, a bowl. When a baby sea turtles reaches adulthood, it will drop a scute.

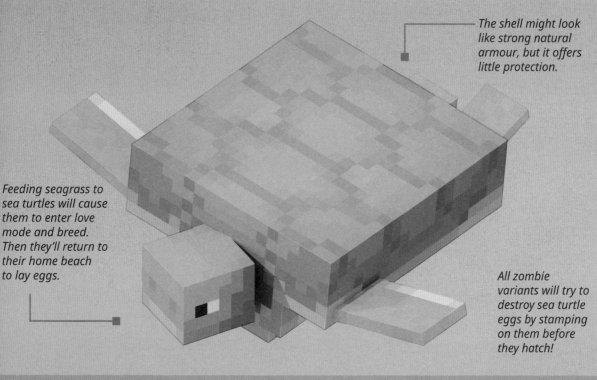

The shell might look like strong natural armour, but it offers little protection.

Feeding seagrass to sea turtles will cause them to enter love mode and breed. Then they'll return to their home beach to lay eggs.

All zombie variants will try to destroy sea turtle eggs by stamping on them before they hatch!

SIZE CHART

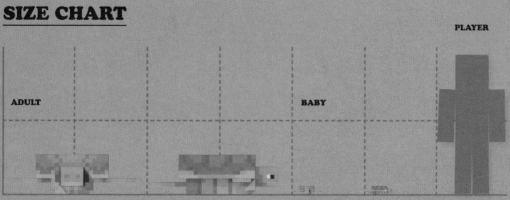

ADULT

BABY

PLAYER

117

TROPICAL FISH

The deep and murky waters of the oceans are probably the last place you'd expect to see a show of vibrant colours, but tropical fish sure put on quite a performance. There are literally thousands of varieties splashing about, filling the Overworld's seas with life and colour. Can you find them all? Er, good luck!

Before discovering tropical fish, I used to make the oceans more colourful by wearing kaleidoscope glasses while swimming. Thank goodness I don't have to do that anymore! What I love about catching tropical fish is that no two schools are ever the same. Well, there's an astronomically small chance they WILL be the same ... but it's not happened yet, and I doubt it will soon! See, there are twenty-two variants a tropical fish can be, but that's just the beginning. Because they can also have a random selection of patterns, sizes, shapes and colours, and so when you factor in all those possibilities ... there are 2,700 varieties! I tried to collect them all, but gave up after 2,699. Oh well.

HABITAT

As their name implies, tropical fish apparently aren't too keen on the cold, so you'll only find them in warm, lukewarm and deep lukewarm ocean biomes. They also appear in lush caves, which makes sense, given their often luscious appearance. They're not too hard to spot, but perhaps consider brewing a potion of Night Vision to help you see more underwater.

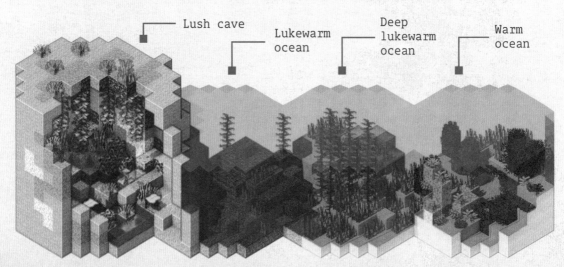

Lush cave

Lukewarm ocean

Deep lukewarm ocean

Warm ocean

■ *Thanks for prettying up the oceans!*

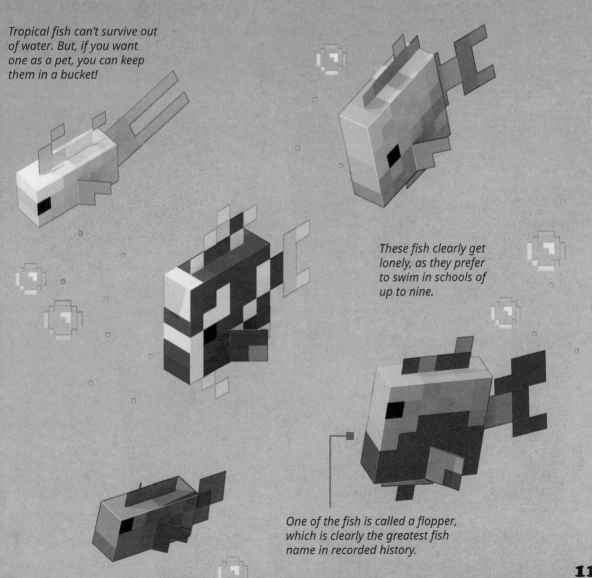

Tropical fish can't survive out of water. But, if you want one as a pet, you can keep them in a bucket!

These fish clearly get lonely, as they prefer to swim in schools of up to nine.

One of the fish is called a flopper, which is clearly the greatest fish name in recorded history.

FROG & TADPOLE

ow does a mob as tiny as the tadpole become something as wonderfully bulbous-necked as the frog? These ribbing rascals hop around the Overworld, scoffing slimes that might otherwise cause you some sticky bother. Although they're rarely in the same dimension, frogs can eat magma cubes – an experience we glowingly recommend you witness!

■

I've always thought frogs look quite smug, especially for a mob that literally eats slime all day. Then again, those slimes do look kinda tasty ... er, what were we talking about again? Oh yes! Fantastic frogs! Did you know that if a frog eats a magma cube, you'll get a froglight block? And that If I try to eat a magma cube, all I get is a burnt tongue? Anyway, froglight blocks are brilliant! They're one of the brightest blocks in the game. Perfect for illuminating your home. Well, so's filling your home with magma cubes, but that's much more dangerous. Trust me.

HABITAT

There are three different colours of frog. You'll find orange frogs spawning naturally in the swamp and mangrove swamp biomes. However, if you want a white or green frog, then you can take tadpoles in a bucket to a biome with a different climate to a swamp and let them grow up there. For a green frog, go to snowy biomes, such as the frozen taiga, or snowy mountains. For white frogs, get your tadpoles to a warmer climate, such as the jungle, desert, or savanna!

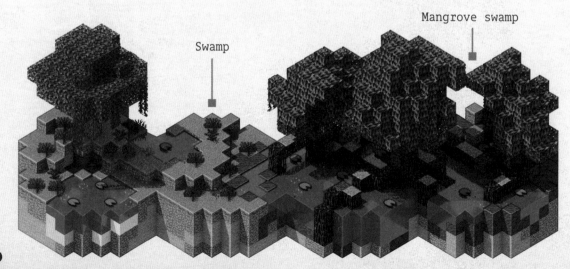

Swamp

Mangrove swamp

■ Hey, save some for us!

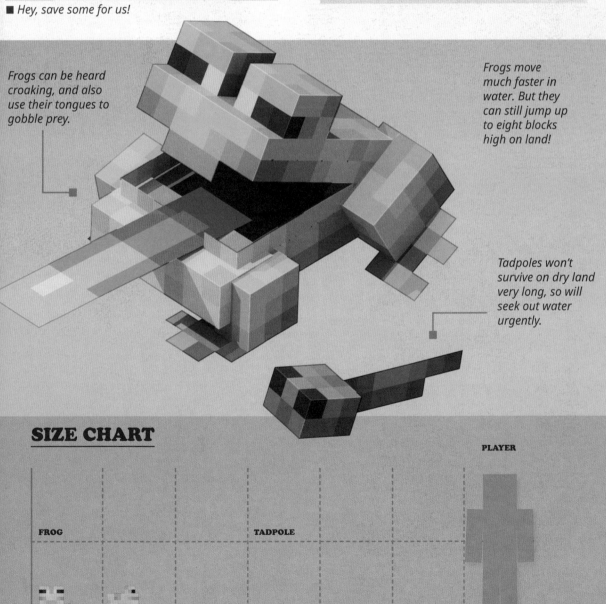

Frogs can be heard croaking, and also use their tongues to gobble prey.

Frogs move much faster in water. But they can still jump up to eight blocks high on land!

Tadpoles won't survive on dry land very long, so will seek out water urgently.

SIZE CHART

PLAYER

FROG

TADPOLE

DOLPHIN

You're in your boat, travelling the Overworld's oceans, when suddenly you get the feeling you're being followed ... by the delightful dolphin! This flippered friend loves the sea, but is also fond of leaping above the waves for a burst of air and to make tourists wish they'd had their camera ready. Missed it again!

> *I've always dreamed of being a successful treasure hunter! If I could just find a buried treasure or two, I'd be rich enough to eat nothing but gold for every meal, and ... well, I can't think of any other examples – but that's OK, because I'd just use my gold to buy some examples! Anyway, here's a little treasure-hunting tip – feed dolphins raw cod or raw salmon, and they'll start swimming away. Give chase! Because their destination is either a shipwreck, buried treasure, or even an ocean ruin. They're leading you to a chest! Why can't all things that you feed raw cod do that? When I fed Heidi Peaks raw cod, she didn't lead me into any treasure, and also said she's never coming to my house for dinner again. Was it something I said?*

HABITAT

You can find dolphins in all the ocean biomes, except the cold ones (so don't bother wrapping up warm and searching for them in the frozen oceans or cold oceans). Then again, perhaps the dolphin will find you? They have been known to chase players who are in boats, so just set sail across the Overworld's oceans and you should soon find several on your tail!

Almost all ocean biomes

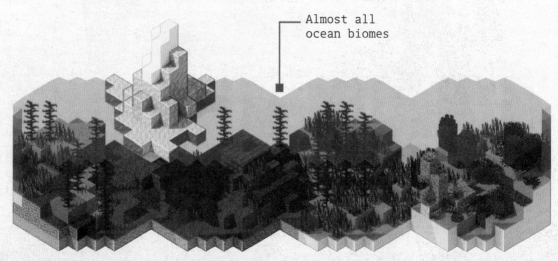

■ *A dolphin leaping from the surface is a truly majestic sight.*

MOB NOTES

OBSERVATIONS: Groups of dolphins are called pods. Pods can contain up to five individual dolphins.

DROPS: Not that you'd want to, but if a dolphin is defeated, it will drop some raw cod – which will be cooked cod if it was defeated with fire.

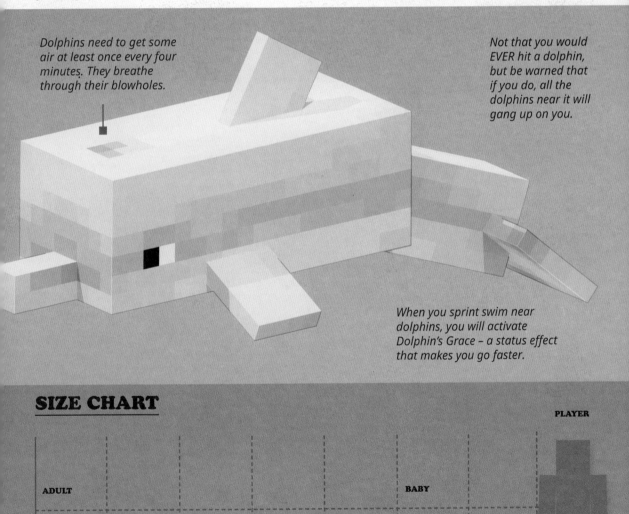

Dolphins need to get some air at least once every four minutes. They breathe through their blowholes.

Not that you would EVER hit a dolphin, but be warned that if you do, all the dolphins near it will gang up on you.

When you sprint swim near dolphins, you will activate Dolphin's Grace – a status effect that makes you go faster.

SIZE CHART

PLAYER

ADULT

BABY

SQUID

The squid could have been one of the sea's most terrifying creatures, a tentacled terror feared by all. Instead, this passive mob prefers a simpler life of just bobbing around the ocean blue, not even interacting with explorers, let alone attacking them. Why don't you follow their example and leave them alone? You can't need their ink sacs THAT badly, even if you're opening a carpet shop and need them for dye, or want to write a book with their ink.

> *As much as I love swimming in the ocean, I used to have a phobia of squid. I don't know why! They're some of the sea's most passive creatures, perfectly content to let me swim by unheeded and ignore my loud whimpering. Once, I was screaming and waving my arms in panic, and I accidentally hit a squid! Next thing I knew, all was darkness. Had I gone blind? Not quite – squid produce a cloud of ink when you attack them! Frankly, I deserved to be coated in ink. In fact, I felt so terrible about what I did to that squid that I baked it a big apology cake! Then I ate the cake by myself. Remind me to bake it a new cake, please!*

HABITAT

Look, do you REALLY need ink sacs? Wandering traders will sell you ink sacs (at rip-off prices, admittedly, but still!). Sometimes you even catch them when fishing! Oh, very well – if you really want to find a squid (for whatever reason you choose), then explore ocean biomes and rivers and you'll soon spot one.

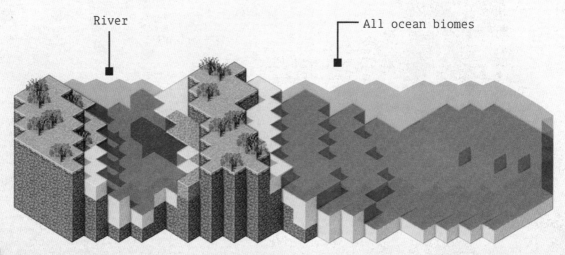

River

All ocean biomes

■ *Wish WE could eject ink when people hit us ...*

MOB NOTES

OBSERVATIONS: Squid have a majestic manner of swimming, moving their tentacles with peaceful purpose. They can even swim effortlessly against a current.
DROPS: A squid defeated by you, guardians or elder guardians will drop up to three ink sacs – a useful item for crafting dye!

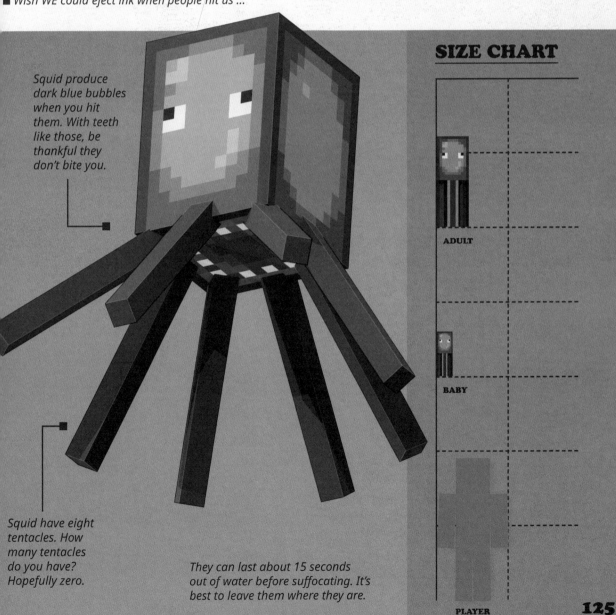

Squid produce dark blue bubbles when you hit them. With teeth like those, be thankful they don't bite you.

Squid have eight tentacles. How many tentacles do you have? Hopefully zero.

They can last about 15 seconds out of water before suffocating. It's best to leave them where they are.

SIZE CHART

ADULT

BABY

PLAYER

125

GLOW SQUID

The squid gets a literal glow-up in the form of this luminescent mob. Sparkling through the darker depths of the Overworld's oceans, the glow squid is so enchanting and pretty that it's easy to ignore the fact it no longer seems to have eyes. Let's ignore that and focus on ooohing and ahhhing at its shiny crystal-like particles instead. Ooooh. Ahhh ...

Great news! This mob is so wonderful, it single-tentaclely cured my phobia of squid! I was swimming in a large body of water I'd found in a cave, when I came across several glow squid. I cleared my throat to help prepare myself to scream with terror. So imagine my surprise when I found myself utterly enchanted instead! Observing this mob is like watching precious gemstones swim through the sea. If only all the other mobs I'm scared of could look like this. Glow spiders! Glow creepers! Actually, both those examples sound terrifying. Forget it!

HABITAT

Glow squid are a lot trickier to track down than normal squid. That's because they only spawn in underground bodies of water. The good news is, they can spawn in ANY water you come across underground. So if you just keep exploring caves and diving into any water you find, you're bound to find a glow squid eventually. They're not exactly hard to spot!

Bodies of water underground

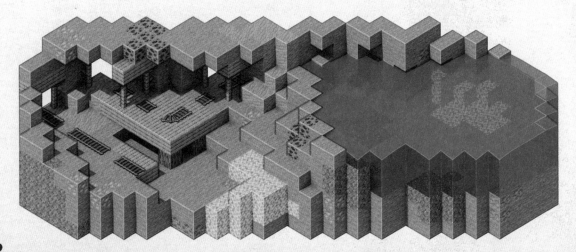

■ *There! Now you can admire this photo of a turquoise ink cloud instead of attacking a glow squid. Hooray!*

MOB NOTES

OBSERVATIONS: It's very unlikely you'll be lucky enough to see a baby glow squid, as they are extremely rare.

DID YOU KNOW?: Glow squid drop glow ink sacs, which you can use as a crafting ingredient. Find some and you can make glowing text on your signs!

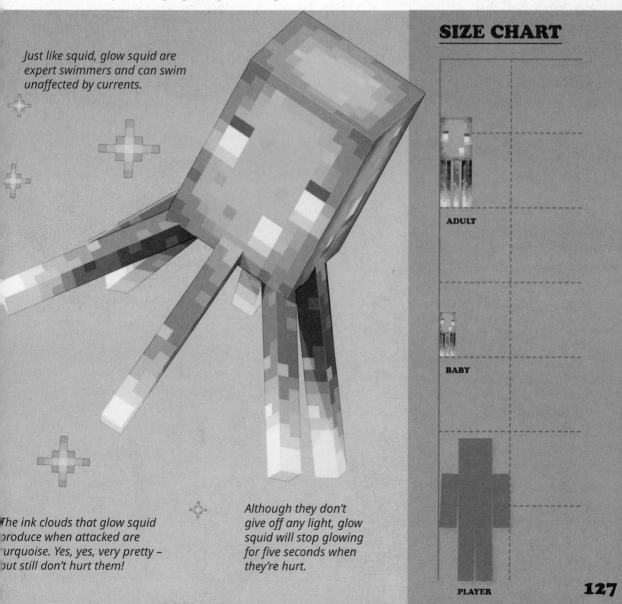

Just like squid, glow squid are expert swimmers and can swim unaffected by currents.

SIZE CHART

ADULT

BABY

PLAYER

The ink clouds that glow squid produce when attacked are turquoise. Yes, yes, very pretty – but still don't hurt them!

Although they don't give off any light, glow squid will stop glowing for five seconds when they're hurt.

127

PUFFERFISH

Proof that even the smallest mobs should never be underestimated, the pufferfish only stays teeny-tiny if you keep your distance. Get up close and it'll start inflating. But fans of living balloons should definitely stay back, because the pufferfish is more than happy to fill you with poison. Dismissing this once-minuscule mob as an airhead would be most unwise indeed ... keep your distance and keep your health!

> Cod and salmon are ever so tasty, but I simply cannot recommend the pufferfish as a seaside snack. When I ate one, I became hungrier, nauseous and poisoned! I was so appalled that I only ate five more. You might think that pufferfish should be avoided at all costs then. Not so! Risky as it is to approach them, they are an important ingredient for brewing a potion of Water Breathing. That's an essential potion if you truly want to explore the Overworld's oceans properly! Now if you'll excuse me, I'm going to try eating another one anyway. No one calls Riley a quitter! Seriously ill, but not a quitter.

HABITAT

Pufferfish spawn in warm and lukewarm ocean biomes, but they're fairly rare. Plus, the fact they're so small makes them tricky to spot. You could always track down an ocean temple and fight guardians and elder guardians. They're two of the Overworld's toughest mobs and they drop a pufferfish on average about 1 in 300 times! Er, actually, maybe just buy a fishing rod?

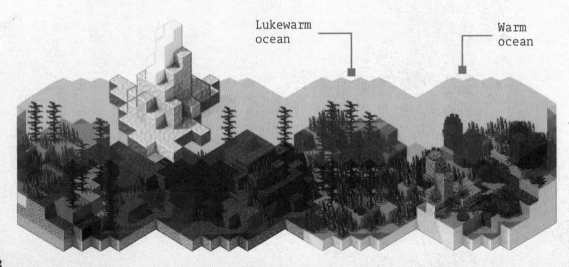

Lukewarm ocean

Warm ocean

■ *Don't be deceived – it'll grow into a bigger, different shape if you get close!*

MOB NOTES

OBSERVATIONS: They are a passive mob which won't cause you any concerns ... Unless, of course, you try to eat one.

DID YOU KNOW?: Pufferfish are found in groups of up to three individuals. While they're small and somewhat difficult to spot, they'll be easier to see once you get closer ...

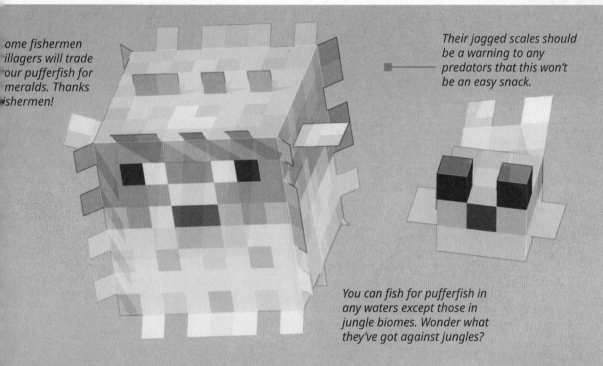

...ome fishermen ...illagers will trade ...our pufferfish for ...meralds. Thanks ...ishermen!

Their jagged scales should be a warning to any predators that this won't be an easy snack.

You can fish for pufferfish in any waters except those in jungle biomes. Wonder what they've got against jungles?

SIZE CHART

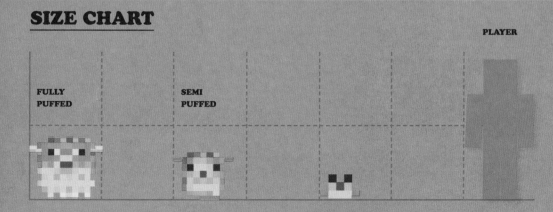

FULLY PUFFED

SEMI PUFFED

PLAYER

DROWNED

What happens when a zombie goes for a swim? It discovers joy in physical fitness and changes its wicked ways forever? Sadly, no. Instead, they become the trident-wielding terrors of the deep known as the drowned. These undersea undead plague the Overworld's oceans and rivers. Fans of not being attacked with tridents should swim with great care ...

Now, call me Riley, but I'm sure the Overworld's oceans would appeal to more swimming enthusiasts if they were populated by only passive mobs. If you've never met a drowned, then you're in for a scare. They're both a constant and nasty nuisance for anyone just trying to enjoy a quiet life under the sea. Keeping your distance isn't even a guarantee of safety, as they're seriously good at throwing tridents at you underwater. But it's their swimming ability that really gets my goat – they're just as fast and flexible at moving through water as I am. So swimming away isn't always the best option. Ow!

HABITAT

Drowned are practically everywhere! They spawn in all ocean biomes, in dripstone cave biomes and river biomes. Basically, if there is lots of water – they could be there. They also occur when zombies have their heads submerged in water for 30 seconds and become drowned. Maybe sticking to dry land isn't such a bad idea after all ...

Almost all bodies of water

Swim! It's gaining on you and we don't think it wants a hug.

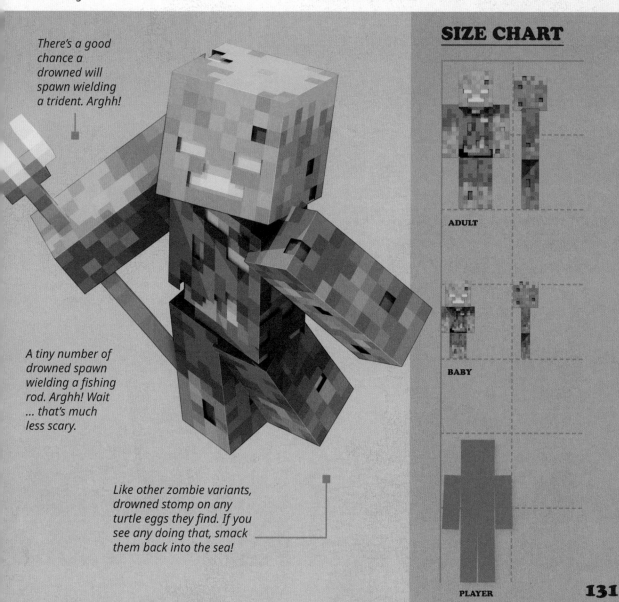

There's a good chance a drowned will spawn wielding a trident. Arghh!

A tiny number of drowned spawn wielding a fishing rod. Arghh! Wait ... that's much less scary.

Like other zombie variants, drowned stomp on any turtle eggs they find. If you see any doing that, smack them back into the sea!

SIZE CHART

ADULT

BABY

PLAYER

GUARDIAN

You don't want to get in the firing line of the guardian's deadly stare. The laser beams they shoot from their eyes are best avoided by any swimmer who enjoys being alive. Those orange spikes on its body can be just as deadly. They aren't decoration or the results of eating a satsuma too sloppily. Get up close and you'll find out just how painful they can be.

> *As someone who's spent their entire adult life trying to bring the monobrow back into fashion, I can't help but respect the guardian. I'd respect it even more if it'd stop shooting laser beams at me. Why can't these GUARDians keep ME safe, eh? If you're a braver diver than I, and are planning to take on a guardian, be warned that its laser attacks are no joke. They can't even be blocked by shields and can hit you from up to 15 blocks away! Basically, this ferocious fish is never not bad news. Nice eyebrow, though. Very striking.*

HABITAT

You'll need to make your way past a guardian to make it inside an ocean monument. These are rare, but can be found in deep ocean biome variants. You'll want to pack plenty of weapons, potions of Water Breathing, food and leave your emeralds safe at home in your chest, before diving deep to find one ...

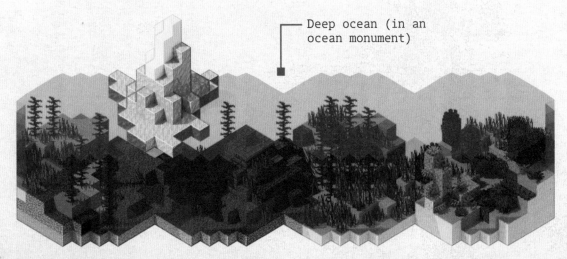

Deep ocean (in an ocean monument)

MOB NOTES

OBSERVATIONS: Guardians appear to have serious issues with anyone that wishes to trespass in an ocean monument.

DID YOU KNOW?: They might be a tough test, but defeated guardians can drop incredibly rare prismarine shards and prismarine crystals. Worth it? YES!

■ *The photographer who took this was never seen again. How unprofessional.*

If there are solid blocks between a guardian's gaze and yourself, it won't fire its laser. So find a wall and get behind it!

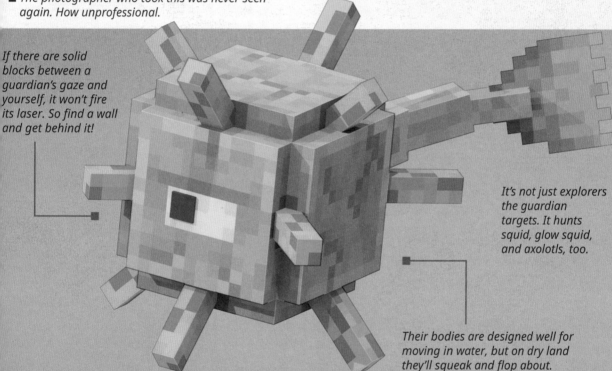

It's not just explorers the guardian targets. It hunts squid, glow squid, and axolotls, too.

Their bodies are designed well for moving in water, but on dry land they'll squeak and flop about.

SIZE CHART

PLAYER

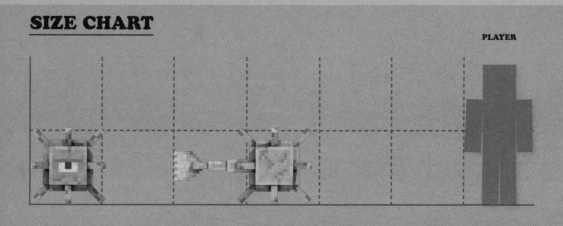

ELDER GUARDIAN

The largest and strongest aquatic mob, few have met the elder guardian and lived to tell the tale (and those survivors tend to tell it while screaming and bursting into tears). The elder guardian is coated in nasty spikes, has an eye laser that's more powerful than a normal guardian and has a third surprise attack that can make mining very difficult indeed ...

> When I first swam into an ocean monument, which is something of an underwater maze, I couldn't help but laugh. Ha! A maze is no challenge in an Overworld where we can mine practically every block away! But the elder guardian got the last laugh, which is impressive, considering it doesn't have a mouth. It blasted me with Mining Fatigue, which dramatically reduces both your mining AND your attack speed. So not only can you not mine your way to safety – you also can't fight back! Luckily, no one moves underwater as rapidly as me, so I was able to dart quickly around until I found a passage out of the monument.

HABITAT

Elder guardians resides in three different locations within ocean monuments, which can occasionally be found in deep ocean biomes. If you're having trouble tracking down one of those, perhaps seek out the skills of a cartographer villager. They'll trade your emeralds for an ocean explorer map that'll point you towards a monument. Thanks, cartographer!

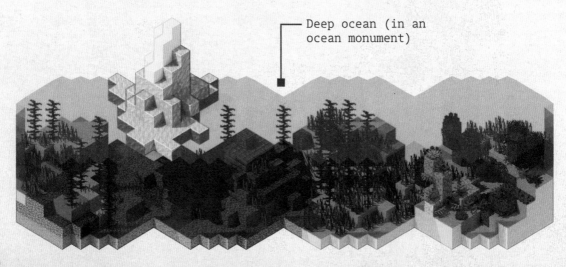

Deep ocean (in an ocean monument)

If you see this happening in the wild, FLEE!

MOB NOTES

OBSERVATIONS: Elder guardians spawn during world creation. Unlike many other mobs, they never respawn.

DROPS: Defeated elder guardians may drop tide armour trim smithing templates, a wet sponge, prismarine shards, prismarine crystals, raw cod or other random fish.

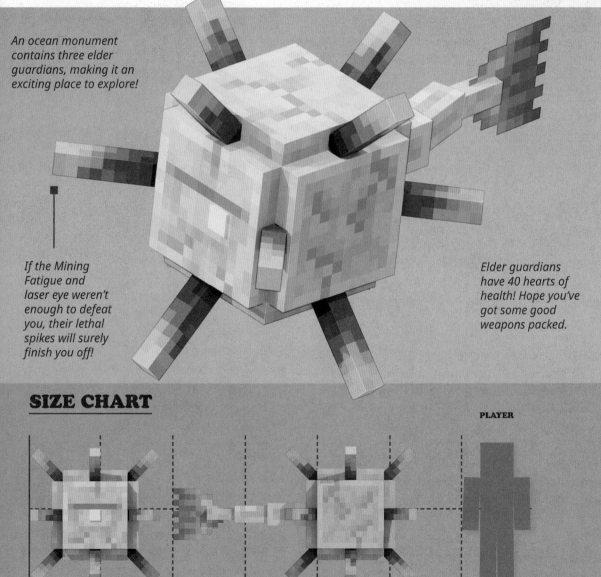

An ocean monument contains three elder guardians, making it an exciting place to explore!

If the Mining Fatigue and laser eye weren't enough to defeat you, their lethal spikes will surely finish you off!

Elder guardians have 40 hearts of health! Hope you've got some good weapons packed.

SIZE CHART

PLAYER

NETHER SPECIALISTS

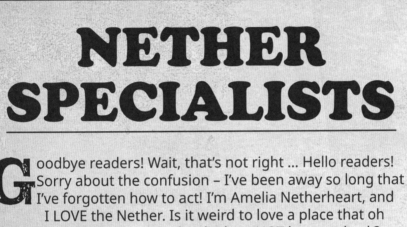

Goodbye readers! Wait, that's not right ... Hello readers! Sorry about the confusion – I've been away so long that I've forgotten how to act! I'm Amelia Netherheart, and I LOVE the Nether. Is it weird to love a place that oh so clearly does NOT love me back? Probably! It's not gonna stop me from foraging its fiery depths, throwing gold at its inhabitants (no, no, trust me, they love it) and cataloguing every mob who resides there.

STRIDER

With an expression that makes a creeper look cheerful, one can only wonder what's made the strider appear so upset. Perhaps being used as a taxi by explorers takes its toll? A shame, as it's the only mob that can be ridden across lava, the strider is an excellent method of getting from A to B without burning up at L, A, V and A.

■

> *When you're a Nether explorer like me, you soon learn that walking on lava is not a good idea. That's why I hop aboard a strider! You'll have to saddle them, but it's worth it for a mob that can walk across lava without burning up. They can be a little aimless in their wandering though, so craft a warped fungus on a stick! Yeah, that isn't appetising to you and me, but you can use them to lead the strider in any direction you want. Wait, why are you leading it back towards the Nether portal? Awww come on, we only just got here!*

HABITAT

Striders spawn in all Nether biomes and can be found on lava. There's lava almost EVERYWHERE in the Nether, so just keep exploring lava-filled areas of it (carefully!) and you're bound to cross paths with a strider eventually (but don't literally cross paths with it – remember, it can walk on lava and you can't!).

All Nether biomes

OBSERVATIONS: These mobs do not like water in any way. Be it rain, or a splash water bottle, they don't react well to it!

DROPS: Defeated striders will always drop at least two string and possibly more. Any that were wearing a saddle will drop that, too – even if you didn't place it on them.

■ Cheer up, strider – only 500 more miles of carrying to go!

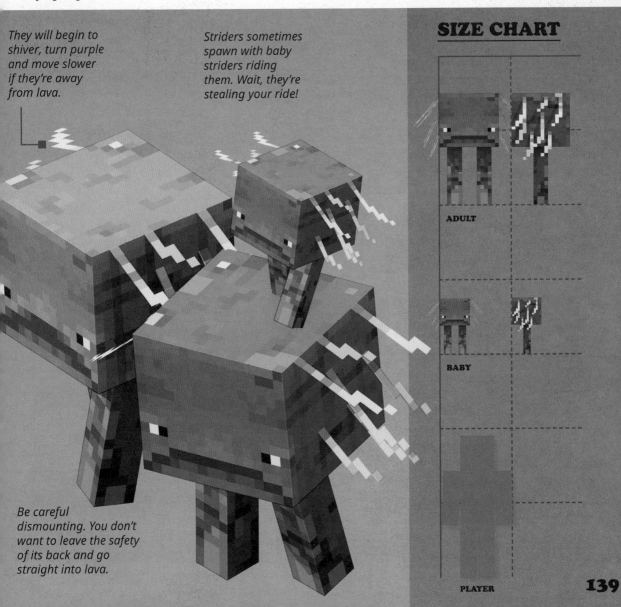

They will begin to shiver, turn purple and move slower if they're away from lava.

Striders sometimes spawn with baby striders riding them. Wait, they're stealing your ride!

Be careful dismounting. You don't want to leave the safety of its back and go straight into lava.

SIZE CHART

ADULT

BABY

PLAYER

PIGLIN

A pig-like being that walks AND is obsessed with the shallow joys of gold. The bling-loving piglin is a mob that will squeal and swing its sword, or fire its crossbow, at any explorer that isn't wearing some golden armour. Dressing in gold may be a little flashy, true, but surely you'd rather wear that than several of this porker's crossbow bolts?

Why do piglins like gold so much? Gold's rubbish! You can't eat it, or plant it, and it gives RUBBISH hugs. Still, since I spend so much time in the Nether, I thought it'd be a good idea to craft myself a golden helmet to keep myself safe from piglins. Did you know that if you're holding a golden item, they'll snort at you? Not a snort of respect either! I think its jealousy! The worst kind of snort there is! That's just one of the reasons I prefer baby piglins. These adorable little piggies are completely passive and will snort at you a bit less. Inspiring!

HABITAT

You'll find piglins in the Nether wastes and the crimson forest biomes, so make sure you've got at least one piece of golden armour on before exploring there. They also spawn in bastion remnants, super-creepy castle-like structures that can appear in all Nether biomes (except for the basalt deltas). So maybe just wear your gold constantly when exploring the Nether. Safety first!

Bastion remnant

Nether wastes

Crimson forest

■ *A piglin doing a celebratory dance! Er, it's lovely.*

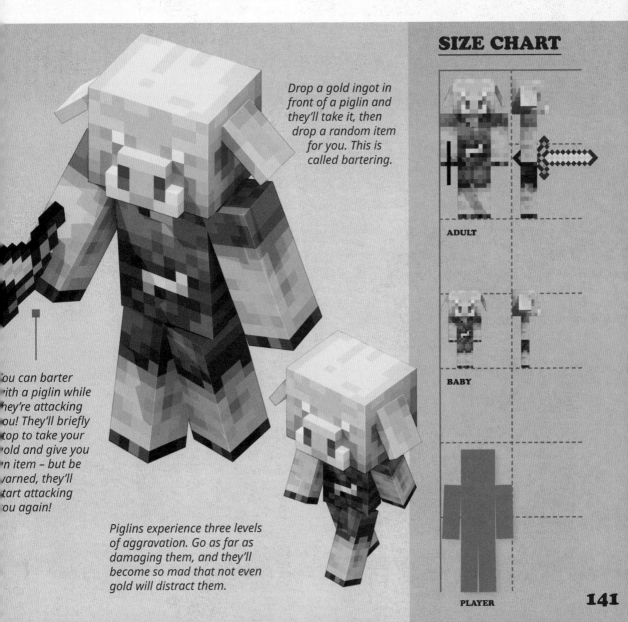

Drop a gold ingot in front of a piglin and they'll take it, then drop a random item for you. This is called bartering.

You can barter with a piglin while they're attacking you! They'll briefly stop to take your gold and give you an item – but be warned, they'll start attacking you again!

Piglins experience three levels of aggravation. Go as far as damaging them, and they'll become so mad that not even gold will distract them.

SIZE CHART

ADULT

BABY

PLAYER

141

PIGLIN BRUTE

Picture the scene – you're enjoying a lovely stroll in the Nether, dressed head to toe in golden armour, confidently strutting because you know piglins don't attack gold-wearers. Suddenly, a larger piglin attacks you! Meet the piglin brute, who doesn't care about your golden fashion sense. The only gold they are interested in, unfortunately, is the golden axe they're swinging at you!

Whoa there, big thing! Piglin brutes are pretty much impossible to negotiate with, and I have the axe scars to prove it. I've tried complimenting their big golden belt, I've tried lobbing gold at their feet, I've even tried snorting nice words at them (uh oh – hope I didn't accidentally snort anything mean ...). Sadly, piglin brutes have no time for debating or bartering. They ALWAYS attack explorers. The only good reason to tangle with one of them is that there's a chance that they'll drop a golden axe. Tempting, but I think I'll try running in the opposite direction for a while instead. See ya!

HABITAT

Well, the good news is that these brutes only spawn in bastion remnants. The bad news is that bastion remnants appear in almost ALL the biomes in the Nether. So make sure that you're on your guard if you do choose to explore those remnants, because wearing gold won't save you now!

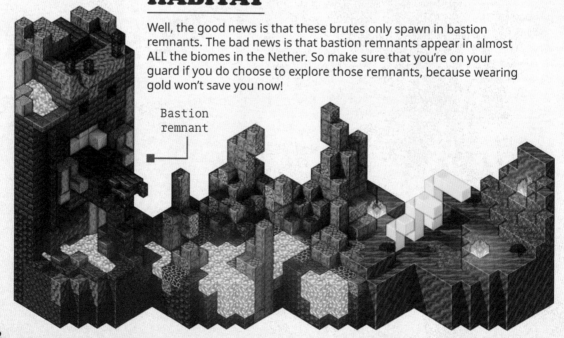

Bastion
remnant

■ Run! They're gaining on you!

Unlike regular piglins, brutes can't wield crossbows. Mildly good news!

Regular piglins do victory dances, but brutes don't care for dancing. How joyless.

Their melee attacks are some of the strongest in the Nether. Try not to find that out for yourself.

SIZE CHART

PLAYER

143

ZOMBIFIED PIGLIN

Perhaps this ham should have spent more time in the fridge? These undead snorters might look hostile, but they're actually neutral. What a relief! However, just like piglins, they love gold and wield golden swords that they'll sometimes drop when defeated.

> OK, they're not the friendliest-looking mob I've ever met. But don't be fooled, because these pigs ain't hostile! Zombified piglins are actually neutral, happy to live their undead lives in peace as long as you leave them alone. Compared to zombies of the Overworld and drowned of the oceans, they are the most peaceful walking corpses around. They're also great for helping you switch to a veggie diet – they may look like pigs but these zombified piglins aren't dropping you a juicy porkchop. Instead, you'll get rotting flesh. And no one wants that with their vegetables!

HABITAT

Zombified piglins spawn naturally in the Nether wastes and crimson forests. The Nether wastes is the most common biome in the Nether, so it won't take you long to find this mob. They've also been known to spawn near Nether portals in the Overworld. Also, keep an eye on your pigs during thunderstorms. If they get struck by lightning, they'll transform into zombified piglins!

Nether wastes

Crimson forest

■ *Uh oh. This pig is about to get a seriously grave makeover ...*

If you attack one, then all nearby zombified piglins will attack you. You have been warned!

Zombified piglins seek out and destroy turtle eggs. Use that sword on something your own size!

If a piglin or piglin brute somehow finds their way into the Overworld or the End, they'll only enjoy their victory for 15 seconds. Then they transform into a zombified piglin.

SIZE CHART

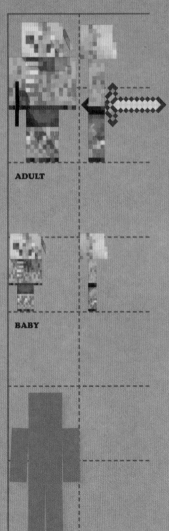

ADULT

BABY

PLAYER

145

HOGLIN & ZOGLIN

hat if the humble pig started hanging out with a bad crowd? Grew out its tusks? Sprouted an unfortunate mohawk? Then started terrorising any adventurer who so much as THINKS about having porkchops for dinner? Yes, the hoglin is aggressive, even before it goes through the zombification process and becomes a zoglin. Rotten!

■

One of the things I love about the Nether is that these adorable hoglins are hostile, whereas the zombified piglins are neutral. Mind you, you'd be pretty hostile too if people kept using you for porkchops and leather! But if you're brave enough to try it, did you know that hoglins are the only hostile mobs you can actually breed? You'll need some crimson fungi, but it's worth it to get some of the most vicious babies in the Nether! Feel free to visit my hoglin farm whenever you like. Just wear some strong armour first. Also, anyone wanna buy a farm from me?

HABITAT

Hoglins sometimes spawn in bastion remnants, but your best bet of finding them is in the crimson forests biome (after all, they can't get enough of that crimson fungi). You'll have to leave the Nether to find yourself a zoglin. When a hoglin enters the Overworld or the End, after 15 seconds, it'll become a zoglin! Er, great?

Crimson forest

MOB NOTES

OBSERVATIONS: They are quite rightfully scared of being hunted by piglins. If they are outnumbered, they'll run away.
DROPS: Defeated hoglins will drop some leather and at least two raw porkchops (cooked if defeated by fire). Zoglins will drop something a bit less tasty ... rotten flesh.

■ *This baby will attack you, but look adorable while doing it. So that's alright then.*

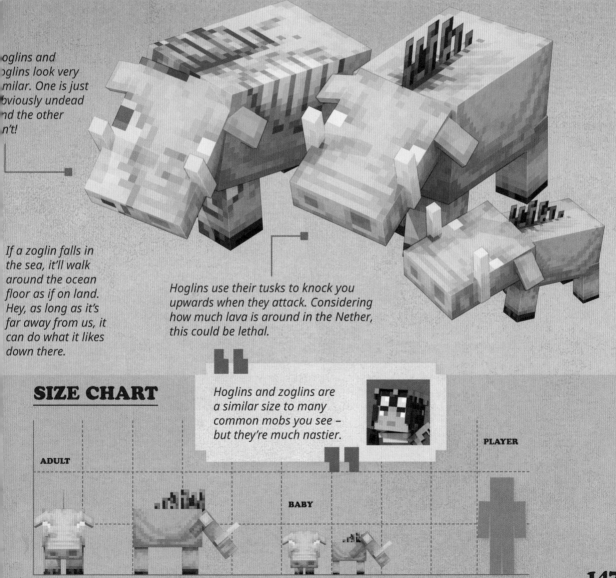

...oglins and ...oglins look very ...milar. One is just ...bviously undead ...nd the other ...n't!

If a zoglin falls in the sea, it'll walk around the ocean floor as if on land. Hey, as long as it's far away from us, it can do what it likes down there.

Hoglins use their tusks to knock you upwards when they attack. Considering how much lava is around in the Nether, this could be lethal.

Hoglins and zoglins are a similar size to many common mobs you see – but they're much nastier.

SIZE CHART

ADULT

BABY

PLAYER

BLAZE

The Nether is a poor choice of holiday destination if you don't like the heat, and few mobs showcase that better than the blaze. Scorching to the touch and fond of lobbing fireballs at explorers, it might make you wish you'd stuck to aquatic biomes. Unfortunately, they are the only way to get blaze rods, a key ingredient in crafting brewing stands!

———————————— ■ ————————————

I have a theory about the blaze. Notice how it looks a bit like a block? I think it knows about all those blocks you've mined in your adventures, and this mob is one of those blocks, back for revenge! OK, this theory is nonsense and probably doesn't hold any water, but I'd highly recommend YOU hold onto some water if you're going blaze-hunting. Actually, pack snowballs and splash water bottles if you really wanna do damage! Ahem, not that I believe in harming any of the lovely mobs in my beloved Nether, of course. But the blaze is pretty deserving.

HABITAT

The good news is that the blaze isn't common in the Nether. They only spawn in Nether fortresses, which, as the name implies, are some of the toughest areas to infiltrate. Especially with these literal hotties hovering around. Unsurprisingly, you won't find many snowballs or splash water bottles in Nether fortresses, so make sure you tool up before exploring them!

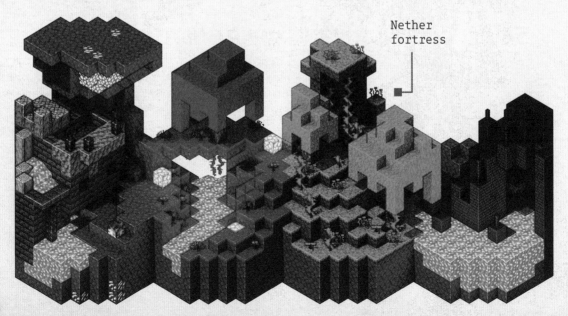

Nether fortress

■ *With its many moving parts, a blaze can be a confusing sight.*

MOB NOTES

OBSERVATIONS: They might not be afraid of most things, but we bet they wouldn't like anything too cold for them, such as thrown snowballs!

DID YOU KNOW?: Defeating a blaze is the only way to gather blaze powder, an essential item for crafting eyes of Ender.

Blazes only shoot fireballs at you when they have a clear line of sight. Quickly, duck behind a block.

This mob takes a lot of damage from powder snow! This would be better news if there was any chance of it snowing in the Nether.

Oddly, its melee attacks aren't considered fire attacks. So, potions of Fire Resistance will only protect you against its launched fireballs.

SIZE CHART

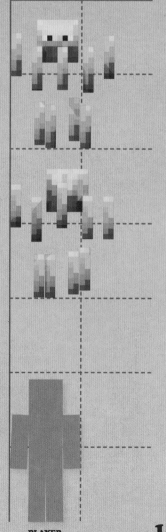

PLAYER

149

GHAST

A terrifying ghost that only a mother could love, which perhaps explains its habit of shrieking like a baby. The ghast strikes almost as much fear into our bones as it does into our ears. Floating around the Nether, these sinister spirits usually have their eyes and mouths clamped shut. You'll miss those days when it does open its mouth and unleashes the horrors within ...

> *Did you know that a ghast's projectile attack could potentially go on forever? It's true! The fireball it shoots out of its ghastly gob won't disappear until it hits something. That means if it somehow spat a fireball into space (yeah, yeah, not likely in the Nether – just go with me on this), that fireball would keep going forever and ever and ever and ever and ever and, well, you get the idea! These are the kind of fun facts I think about to keep my spirits up when these mean spirits are shooting exploding fireballs right into my face. Why are YOU the one crying like a baby, ghast? I'm the one who just got a face full of flames!*

HABITAT

Ghasts are easy to find – their piercing shrieks can be heard from up to 80 blocks away. You'll find them wailing in the basalt deltas, Nether wastes and soul sand valley biomes. Imagine waking up every morning to those screams ... no wonder you'll never see a villager on vacation here.

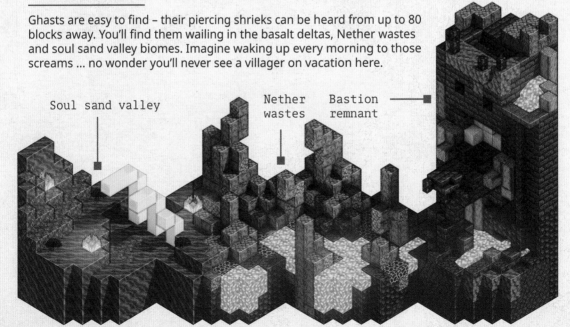

Soul sand valley

Nether wastes

Bastion remnant

■ *A spit-based fire attack? What a gross way to go!*

MOB NOTES

OBSERVATIONS: If you've caused damage to a ghast, it will target you from up to 64 blocks away. Run ... RUUUUNNN!

DROPS: A defeated ghast (good luck with that!) could drop some gunpowder, and a ghast tear – a rare item used to craft potions of Regeneration and End crystals.

Ghasts can be set on fire but also take NO fire damage. Er, perhaps try a different combat strategy then?

Ghast tears are a crucial ingredient for potions of Regeneration. We'll leave it to you to decide whether that's worth risking a battle.

If they're too close when attacking, ghasts can be hurt by their own fireballs. Ha! Oh, wait, we still got hurt too.

SIZE CHART

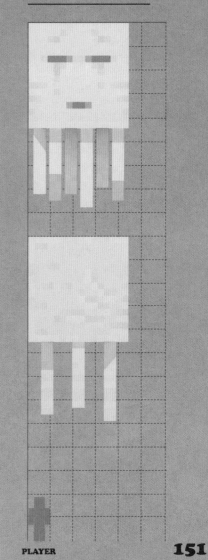

MAGMA CUBE

Hot, angry squares that multiply when you destroy them, the magma cube is a small mob that can quickly become a big problem. Many visitors to the Nether have underestimated these bouncing blocks and that's why they were never seen again. They are similar to slimes, except that magma cubes jump higher, hit harder and are irritatingly immune to fire. Yikes. Slimes, all is forgiven!

———————————— ■ ————————————

> *I knew it! I knew the blocks would rise up and fight back eventually! That's why every time I ever mined a block in the Overworld, I always loudly said how sorry I was and sent all the surrounding blocks flowers. Sure, it took me forever, but who's laughing now? Well, everyone. At me. Because the magma cube couldn't care less about my apologies. It just wants to jump on any explorer it sees! At least when it's mid-jump it looks a bit like the middle of an accordion, which is a nice image to enjoy before all the pain of it landing on me kicks in.*

HABITAT

Oh dear. These crazy-hot cubes spawn in all Nether biomes, though they are more common in some biomes than others. If you're in the basalt deltas, you're bound to cross paths with them, whereas they're somewhat rarer in Nether wastes. Luckily, they're not too hard to spot.

All Nether biomes

■ *A magma cube enjoying some jumping!*

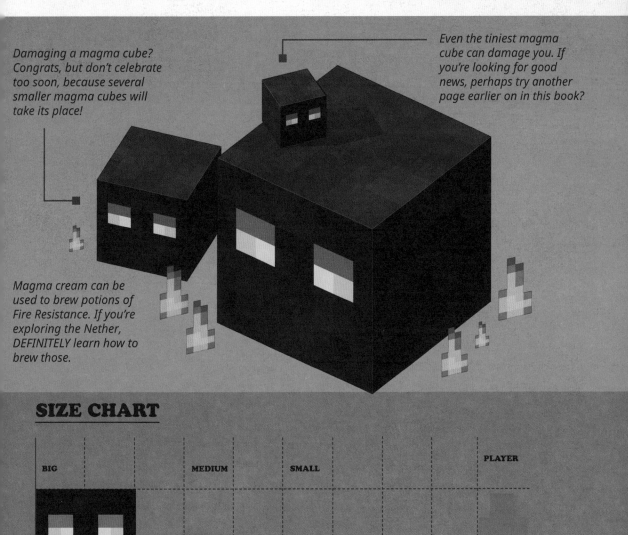

Damaging a magma cube? Congrats, but don't celebrate too soon, because several smaller magma cubes will take its place!

Even the tiniest magma cube can damage you. If you're looking for good news, perhaps try another page earlier on in this book?

Magma cream can be used to brew potions of Fire Resistance. If you're exploring the Nether, DEFINITELY learn how to brew those.

SIZE CHART

BIG MEDIUM SMALL PLAYER

WITHER SKELETON

Some might argue that a living skeleton is plenty scary already. FOOLS! For they clearly haven't crossed paths with the taller, faster, stone-sword-swinging Wither skeleton. Capable of inflicting the poison-like Wither effect, you'd better bash these bones before they strike you down first.

I love living in the Nether! H-honest! It's just, now I think about it, maybe I picked the wrong part of the book to go all-in on? I mean, Addie Venture gets to spend her pages hanging out with lovely sheep. Meanwhile, here I am with the Wither skeleton, a mob that's such poor company that it makes you wish you WERE getting poisoned! The Wither effect is worse than poison, because it turns your health bar black, so you can't see how much health you have left! I try to see the best in every mob, and I'll try to start seeing the best in the Wither skeleton, as soon as it stops smacking me ...

HABITAT

Luckily, Wither skeletons aren't just wandering around all the Nether biomes. You'll only find them if you're brave or stupid enough to explore a Nether fortress. However, the mob that you're unfortunately going to meet when you turn the page is capable of spawning more Wither skeletons. Bet you miss the regular skeletons of the Overworld now, eh?

Nether
fortress

■ *These jerks are hard to defeat thanks to their immunity to fire damage.*

MOB NOTES

OBSERVATIONS: Any spiders spawned in the Nether have a small chance of having a Wither skeleton on their back.

DROPS: There is a chance a defeated Wither skeleton will drop a Wither skeleton skull, as well as coal, bones and even their enchanted stone sword.

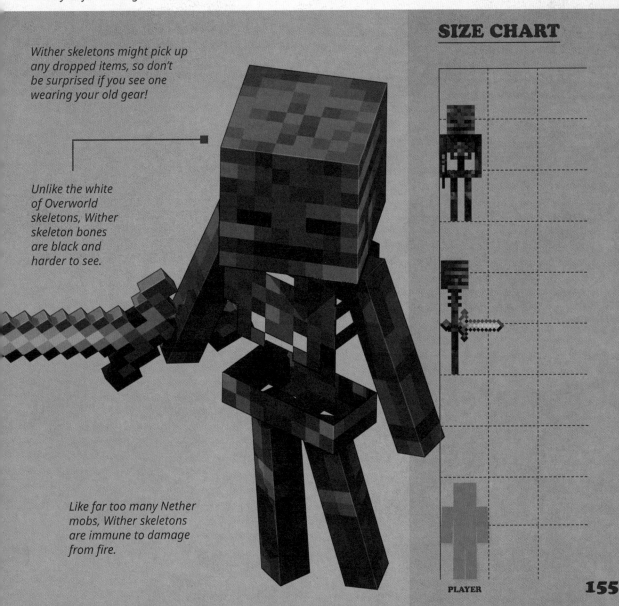

Wither skeletons might pick up any dropped items, so don't be surprised if you see one wearing your old gear!

Unlike the white of Overworld skeletons, Wither skeleton bones are black and harder to see.

Like far too many Nether mobs, Wither skeletons are immune to damage from fire.

SIZE CHART

PLAYER

WITHER

A boss mob of incredible power and a stark reminder that three heads are only better than one when all three of those heads don't wish you immense harm. The Wither should only be summoned by the bravest of players who really want to get their hands on a Nether star to craft a beacon. This terrifying mob introduces itself by exploding. Nice to meet you, too!

> The Wither is one of the very few mobs that you have to construct yourself. There's even a clue about what you need to do in one of the paintings you can make and hang! Not that I recently snuck through a Nether portal and returned to the safety of the Overworld, hahahaha ... Ahem, anyway, you'll need four soul sand/ soul soil blocks and three Wither skeleton skulls. Luckily, I have tons of Wither skeleton skulls lying around (don't ask why), so I was able to summon this mob in no time! But less luckily, I also remembered only AFTER summoning it that the Wither is a terrifying beast that's best not summoned at all. Arghhh! Bye readers! Remember me as someone who only made a few thousand mistakes!

HABITAT

Well, considering you build it yourself, its habitat can be wherever you like (might we suggest 'nowhere at all'?). But to get the soul sand/soul soil, you should visit soul sand valleys or Nether wastes (soul sand can also be found in ancient cities, if you don't fancy a trip to the Nether). Wither skeleton skulls are dropped by Wither skeletons in Nether fortresses. Good luck!

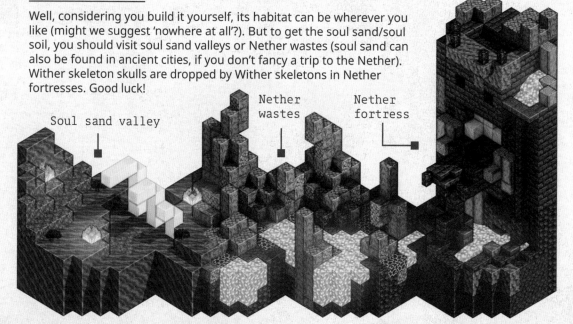

Soul sand valley

Nether wastes

Nether fortress

■ *The painting that hints at how to build the Wither. No hints of how horrible it is, mind ...*

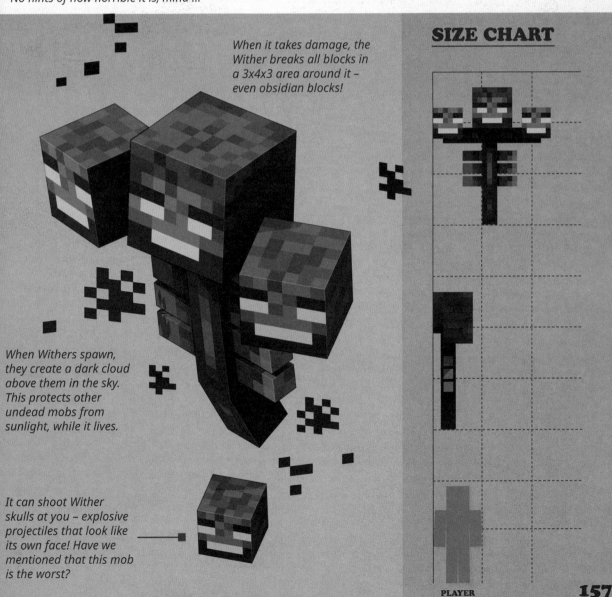

When it takes damage, the Wither breaks all blocks in a 3x4x3 area around it – even obsidian blocks!

SIZE CHART

When Withers spawn, they create a dark cloud above them in the sky. This protects other undead mobs from sunlight, while it lives.

It can shoot Wither skulls at you – explosive projectiles that look like its own face! Have we mentioned that this mob is the worst?

PLAYER

157

END EXPERTS

Eureka! I've discovered a reader! OK, true, not the most amazing scientific discovery of all time ... But that's why I, Professor Ed Portale, spend so much time in the End! Though to be honest, I can't really remember WHY I came to this scary dimension in the first place. Scientific research? I lost my scute collection? Trying to make friends? Well, whatever the reason, I'm glad I did! The End may be terrifying and dangerous, but it's also full of fascinating mobs. I can honestly say I've never been more scientifically satisfied! So keep your guard up, hop into that End portal and join me for the final chapter of the book. It'll be terminal! I mean, it'll be fun!

ENDERMAN

Fans of making eye contact should look away now. Because the Enderman doesn't appreciate anyone looking into its perplexing purple eyes. This lanky mob moves around carrying blocks and prefers doing this without being observed. It'll get hostile very quickly with anyone who dares meet its stare. Don't underestimate their scrawny limbs. They can finish you off in the blink of an eye.

> *What a fascinating creature! I'd love to catalogue it for this page, but I've been told that looking at it is not a good idea. Pah! I'm sure a quick peek couldn't hurt ... oh my! It's even prettier than I'd dared to dream! True, right after I looked at the Enderman, it teleported and hit me in the back, but that's a small price to pay to gaze upon this beautiful beast. Endermen will stay neutral so long as you keep your eyes away from theirs. They're also one of the rare mobs that can pick up blocks, including ones I've used for my house. Hey, stop griefing!*

HABITAT

Despite the slightly misleading name, you don't actually have to visit the End to meet an Enderman. It's one of many mobs that stalk the biomes of the Overworld during nightfall. They can also spawn in the Nether and in (surprise!) the End. This makes them the only mob that can naturally spawn in all three dimensions!

The Overworld

The Nether

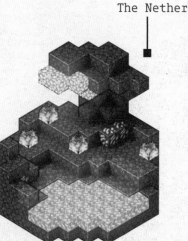

The End

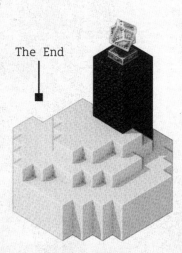

■ *Give that back. Pick up one of my less valuable blocks!*

If you wear a carved pumpkin and look at an Endermen through that, it won't become hostile. What a tasty loophole!

You need Ender pearls to get to the End. So if you want to visit this dreadful dimension, you're going to have to fight some Endermen.

SIZE CHART

Don't waste your time with ranged attacks – it will just teleport away before the projectile can hit it.

PLAYER

161

ENDERMITE

It may be the smallest hostile mob there is, but the teeny-tiny terror that is the endermite still shouldn't be underestimated. A biting attack that only takes off one heart of damage may seem like a small threat, but this mob is so minuscule that it can easily take you by surprise and it won't stop at just one bite. Plus, if you were to be defeated by something so puny, you'd be so humiliated that you'd never live it down back in the Overworld.

◼

> *Ever used an Ender pearl? They're rather brilliant. Throw them and you'll teleport to the spot where they land. Great news for me, a scientist who much prefers teleporting to walking or ever getting up from the sofa. But sadly, Ender pearls come with a couple of downsides. First off, when you use them, you take five hearts of fall damage. Ouch! Plus, when you use an Ender pearl, there's a 5% chance that an endermight mite appear! I mean, an endermite might appear! If you've just taken five hearts of fall damage, even something as minuscule as the endermite could potentially finish you off, so use those Ender pearls cautiously!*

HABITAT

Endermites will only spawn when you use an Ender pearl to teleport, which are obtained through defeating Endermen or trading with villagers or piglins. As you can technically use Ender pearls in any dimension, it means that endermites can spawn anywhere.

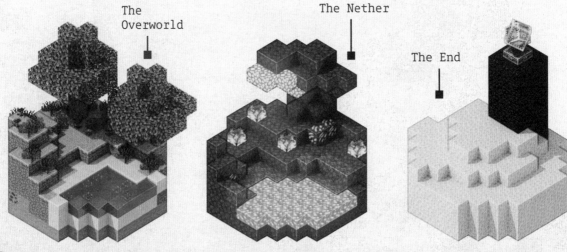

The Overworld

The Nether

The End

MOB NOTES

OBSERVATIONS: Surprisingly, despite their similar names, Endermen are hostile towards endermites.

DID YOU KNOW?: There is a small chance an endermite will spawn every time you throw an Ender pearl. Look out! They're so small, you may not notice when they do.

■ *An Enderman attacking an endermite. Really? Can't we all just get along? No? OK!*

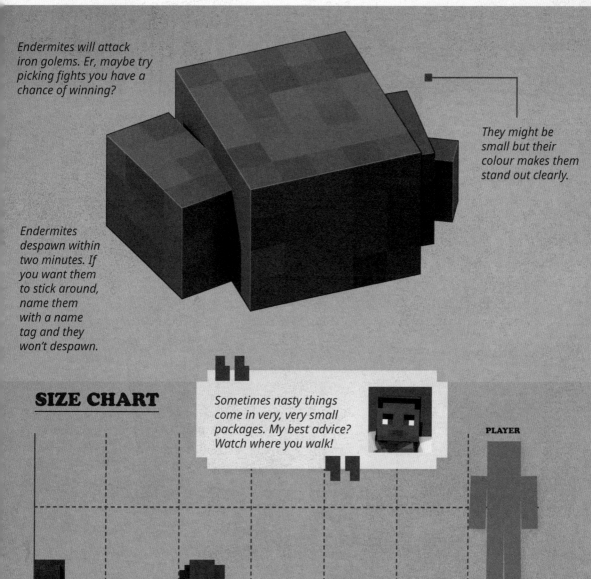

Endermites will attack iron golems. Er, maybe try picking fights you have a chance of winning?

They might be small but their colour makes them stand out clearly.

Endermites despawn within two minutes. If you want them to stick around, name them with a name tag and they won't despawn.

SIZE CHART

Sometimes nasty things come in very, very small packages. My best advice? Watch where you walk!

PLAYER

163

SHULKER

Did that block just ... move? You may be in the presence of a shulker, because their shell looks irritatingly similar to a purpur block. But where the delightful purpur block adds a welcome splash of purple to your builds, the shulker prefers to fill you with bullets and send you flying. Quite literally, as a shulker bullet inflicts damage and Levitation. Try to stay on guard AND on the ground!

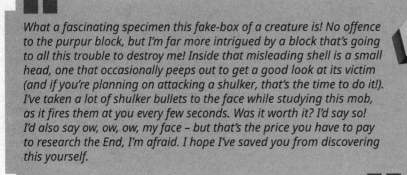

What a fascinating specimen this fake-box of a creature is! No offence to the purpur block, but I'm far more intrigued by a block that's going to all this trouble to destroy me! Inside that misleading shell is a small head, one that occasionally peeps out to get a good look at its victim (and if you're planning on attacking a shulker, that's the time to do it!). I've taken a lot of shulker bullets to the face while studying this mob, as it fires them at you every few seconds. Was it worth it? I'd say so! I'd also say ow, ow, ow, my face – but that's the price you have to pay to research the End, I'm afraid. I hope I've saved you from discovering this yourself.

HABITAT

You'll find shulkers if you defeat the Ender dragon and reveal a portal to explore an End city. These bizarre structures contain treasures for anyone who dares explore inside. If you're lucky (or unlucky), you might just find a purpur block that isn't what it seems ...

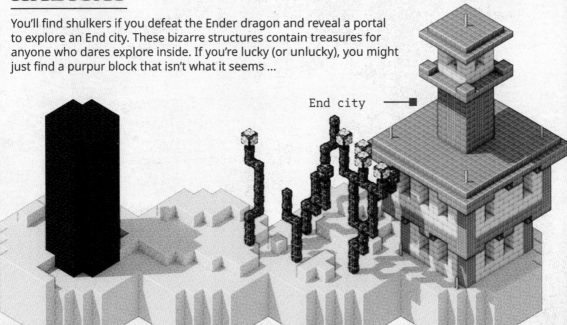

End city ────■

■ *One of these blocks is not like the others ...*

After it takes a certain amount of damage, shulkers sometimes teleport away. Hey, come back! No fair!

Not a fan of purple? Then you can dye a shulker shell different colours!

A shulker bullet inflicts Levitation on you for ten seconds. Wait ... how is giving us the power of flight a punishment? Oh the fall damage, I see.

SIZE CHART

PLAYER

165

ENDER DRAGON

An enormous flying mob of immense power, the Ender Dragon is the ultimate challenge for only the most hardcore explorers. If you've ended up in the End, then you're not leaving until you face this ferocious fire-breather. This is a mob so awesome it even has its own theme music. Do you have any idea how terrifying you have to be to get your own theme music? Extremely!

Most explorers go their entire lives without meeting the Ender Dragon. Indeed, when I invited all the other contributors to this book to come meet the dragon with me, they all RSVPd 'go away'. Bah! Who needs them? Not when I get this glorious dragon all to myself! True, the dragon fireballs it keeps pelting me with are excruciatingly painful, but look how much I'm learning from the pretty purple clouds that they produce! I'm learning things like 'these purple clouds inflict damage, ow'. Fascinating! You can even bottle them up to get dragon's breath, although perhaps I should focus on the fight if I want to make it through relatively unscathed ... Wish me luck, reader, and thanks for joining me in the End!

HABITAT

The Ender Dragon spawns in the End, seconds after you arrive there. As tough as it is to get everything you need to reach The End, it's probably for the best that you can't find the Ender Dragon anywhere else. Imagine if they spawned all across the Overworld? The pain, the horror!

The End

MOB NOTES

OBSERVATIONS: The mighty Ender Dragon won't accept you trying to destroy its End crystals. It uses these to heal itself.

DID YOU KNOW?: Once defeated, the Ender Dragon is gone. For good. Unless you place four End crystals around the exit portal ... Hey, what are you doing? Nooo!

■ We battled the Ender Dragon 34 times before we were able to get the perfect shot. You're welcome.

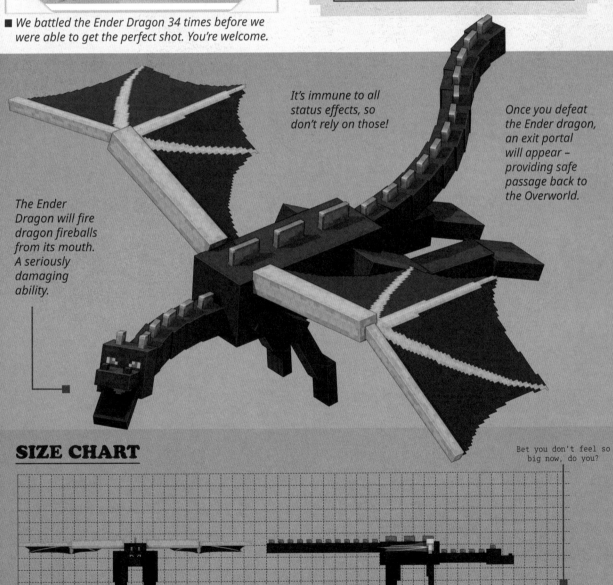

It's immune to all status effects, so don't rely on those!

Once you defeat the Ender dragon, an exit portal will appear – providing safe passage back to the Overworld.

The Ender Dragon will fire dragon fireballs from its mouth. A seriously damaging ability.

SIZE CHART

Bet you don't feel so big now, do you?

GOODBYE

Wow, what a ride! Those explorers certainly know their creepers from their screamer goats! We may have reached the end of this journey – but we have a feeling your adventure is just getting started.

So, which mobs will you track down first? Whether you're roaming the Overworld's plains, mining in its deep caves, treading carefully (or running away) in the Nether or exploring the End dimension, only you can decide where you'll go next. Your adventure is what you make it.

Remember, you can always refer to this guide to help you on your way. But we've seen enough to believe that you've got what it takes to become a legendary Mobspotter!

– MOJANG STUDIOS

INDEX

INDEX

INDEX